THE COMPLETE
IDIOT'S
GUIDE® TO

W9-BPM-896

# Piano Exercises

by Karen Berger

ALPHA

A member of Penguin Group (USA) Inc.

**ALPHA BOOKS**

Published by the Penguin Group

Penguin Group (USA) Inc., 375 Hudson Street, New York, New York 10014, USA

Penguin Group (Canada), 90 Eglinton Avenue East, Suite 700, Toronto, Ontario M4P 2Y3, Canada (a division of Pearson Penguin Canada Inc.)

Penguin Books Ltd., 80 Strand, London WC2R 0RL, England

Penguin Ireland, 25 St. Stephen's Green, Dublin 2, Ireland (a division of Penguin Books Ltd.)

Penguin Group (Australia), 250 Camberwell Road, Camberwell, Victoria 3124, Australia (a division of Pearson Australia Group Pty. Ltd.)

Penguin Books India Pvt. Ltd., 11 Community Centre, Panchsheel Park, New Delhi—110 017, India

Penguin Group (NZ), 67 Apollo Drive, Rosedale, North Shore, Auckland 1311, New Zealand (a division of Pearson New Zealand Ltd.)

Penguin Books (South Africa) (Pty.) Ltd., 24 Sturdee Avenue, Rosebank, Johannesburg 2196, South Africa

Penguin Books Ltd., Registered Offices: 80 Strand, London WC2R 0RL, England

International Standard Book Number: 978-1-61564-049-2
Library of Congress Catalog Card Number: 2010908791

13   12            8   7   6   5   4   3

Interpretation of the printing code: The rightmost number of the first series of numbers is the year of the book's printing; the rightmost number of the second series of numbers is the number of the book's printing. For example, a printing code of 11-1 shows that the first printing occurred in 2011.

*Printed in the United States of America*

**Note:** This publication contains the opinions and ideas of its author. It is intended to provide helpful and informative material on the subject matter covered. It is sold with the understanding that the author and publisher are not engaged in rendering professional services in the book. If the reader requires personal assistance or advice, a competent professional should be consulted.

The author and publisher specifically disclaim any responsibility for any liability, loss, or risk, personal or otherwise, which is incurred as a consequence, directly or indirectly, of the use and application of any of the contents of this book.

Most Alpha books are available at special quantity discounts for bulk purchases for sales promotions, premiums, fund-raising, or educational use. Special books, or book excerpts, can also be created to fit specific needs.

For details, write: Special Markets, Alpha Books, 375 Hudson Street, New York, NY 10014.

**Publisher:** *Marie Butler-Knight*
**Associate Publisher:** *Mike Sanders*
**Senior Managing Editor:** *Billy Fields*
**Acquisitions Editor:** *Karyn Gerhard*
**Development Editor:** *Ginny Munroe*
**Production Editor:** *Kayla Dugger*
**Copy Editor:** *Christine Hackerd*
**Cover Designer:** *Kurt Owens*
**Book Designers:** *William Thomas, Rebecca Batchelor*
**Indexer:** *Tonya Heard*
**Layout:** *Brian Massey*
**Proofreader:** *John Etchison*

*This book is dedicated to my teachers and my students, in the hope that it helps pass the knowledge I have been given from one generation of musicians to the next.*

# Contents

# Introduction

How would you like to sit down at the piano and just let your fingers shimmer up and down the keyboard in a glistening arpeggio? Maybe there's a piece by Mozart or Chopin that you've always wanted to play, but it just seems that you'll never be able to wrap your fingers around those octaves or jumping chords. Maybe there's a pounding blues passage you want to add to your repertoire, or a challenging rhythmic riff.

Of course, you already know that practice makes perfect. But what kind of practice?

Practicing technical exercises needn't take more than a few minutes a day. But by zeroing in on those elements that you need to learn to play your favorite music, you can get basic techniques firmly in hand. When you encounter these patterns in music, you're all ready to go.

This book is your toolbox. Most pianists have a few reliable tools: a scale here, an arpeggio there. This book assumes that if you have better tools, you can do a better job, and it gives you those tools with scores of musical examples of scales, chords, arpeggios, riffs, and techniques ranging from playing subtle dynamics to pounding out keyboard-shaking double-octaves.

I assume you can already read music. Beyond that, this book is appropriate for all levels of recreational pianists. Beginners may want to stay in Parts 1 and 2 for a while, while more advanced players will head for Parts 3 and 4. There's a lot of flexibility here. Advanced players can adapt the exercises earlier in the book to make them more difficult (you'll find suggestions for doing so throughout the book). And by reading the explanations in Parts 3 and 4, newer players can get an idea of practice strategies, musical issues, and what lies ahead.

## What You'll Find in This Book

**Part 1, The Basics,** covers the basics. If you're a beginner, start here. But even more advanced players may pick up some pointers, particularly about fingering (some of you missed that lesson the first time around) and basic hand positions.

In **Part 2, Moving Along,** I cover the fundamentals of scales: the major "Do Re Mi" scale, minor scales, chromatic scales, whole-tone scales, blues scales, and modes. I talk about how scales are actually used in music, and give you ideas that combine practicing scales with improvisation. Scales may be the building blocks of music, but there's no reason they should be boring.

**Part 3, Scaling the Heights,** focuses on scales, scales, and more scales. These patterns are the building blocks of technique, composition, and improvisation. By mastering them, you'll develop a firm grasp of keyboard geography. I cover the well-known major scales, of course, as well as minor scales, modes, blues scales, chromatic scales, and more.

**Part 4, Practice Skills,** focuses on how to get the most out of your practice. I start with the essentials of using a metronome. Using a metronome goes way beyond checking your speed: playing exercises in a rhythmic groove helps your technique. I also teach you how to use the famous Hanon exercises (a staple of piano technique for the last 100 years) to help you with transposing, fluency in finding and playing chords, and developing hand independence.

**Part 5, Advanced Skills,** covers the skills needed to play bigger, more complex pieces. Fingering techniques aren't always obvious; I'll show you some of the secrets to getting through a passage that seems to require 20 fingers when you have only 10. I also cover advanced scale techniques that really wow an audience, with exercises to help you learn to play blazing octaves, broken octaves, and scales in different intervals. Arpeggio fingerings are also covered, to help you shimmer up and down the piano. I've also added a chapter on challenging rhythms and ornamentation ranging from Baroque trills and turns to bluesy glissandi.

## Using the CD

This book includes written-out musical examples and exercises, along with a CD. Throughout the book, you'll find an icon that looks like this:

 This icon indicates that the musical example shown or described in the text is on the audio CD. Not all the musical exercises are recorded. (You didn't really need to hear the major scale played in *all* 12 keys, did you?) But if you find yourself wondering how in the world a certain exercise is supposed to sound, chances are it's on the CD.

Most of the examples on the CD are demonstration tracks that show you how an exercise should be practiced. In some cases, metronome suggestions are given, but you should feel free to play slower, if necessary. (Slow and correct is always preferable to fast and sloppy.)

The CD also contains a few play-along tracks, with which you are encouraged to improvise, using scales you have learned in the book. These examples all include sample improvisations followed by a chord-and-click track, over which you can make up your own music. You'll have a measure's worth of clicks to cue you in.

In some cases, tracks may contain more than one musical exercise, especially when the examples cover closely related subjects. Appendix A contains a list of all the tracks and their contents, along with timing cues for tracks that contain multiple exercises.

## Extras

This book also contains tips, warnings, and interesting bits and pieces of information. You'll find four kinds of sidebars:

**FLYING FINGERS**

These sidebars provide quick and easy advice about a particular technical issue raised in the chapter. They are intended to give specific examples of what is described in the text.

**SOUR NOTES**

These sidebars highlight various mistakes that pianists might make—and the consequences.

**THEORY AND PRACTICE**

The whys and hows of technique are often intriguing. These boxes delve into interesting footnotes that help you think about the exercises and your practice regimen.

**UNIVERSAL LANGUAGE**

Music might be the universal language, but it's got quite a few arcane, interesting, and just plain weird terms. Some have an interesting story behind them, and some of them need a bit of translation.

## Acknowledgments

Thanks to my editor Karyn Gerhard. It's not every day a music writer gets an editor who is also a musician, and this is the second time I've benefitted from Karyn's in-depth knowledge of and love for music.

I'd also like to thank the Alpha team, who had the challenging job of putting together a manuscript that includes technical text, musical examples, and a CD: development editor Ginny Bess Munroe, production editor Kayla Dugger, layout technician Brian Massey, and proofreader John Etchison.

Thanks also to Marilyn Allen, my agent, for her business acumen and continued support over the last three years and three books.

I cannot imagine a better recording experience than working on this CD at Off the Beat-n-Track Studio in Sheffield, Massachusetts. Todd Mack smoothed the process of keeping this project on schedule, and recording engineer Will Curtiss has the rare combination of tact and good ears (and he's fun to work with, too).

And finally, thanks to David Hodge, author of *The Complete Idiot's Guide to Playing Bass Guitar*, *The Complete Idiot's Guide to Playing Rock Guitar*, and *The Complete Idiot's Guide to Guitar*. David blazed the trail of learning how to work on these complex books, and I got the benefit of his experience.

## Trademarks

All terms mentioned in this book that are known to be or are suspected of being trademarks or service marks have been appropriately capitalized. Alpha Books and Penguin Group (USA) Inc. cannot attest to the accuracy of this information. Use of a term in this book should not be regarded as affecting the validity of any trademark or service mark.

# The Basics

When you start taking piano lessons, you might see similarities to a golf lesson or a yoga class: the instructor is telling you to do seemingly impossible things with one part of your body while holding another part of your body in an equally impossible position (and relax while you're at it).

Playing the piano has a lot in common with athletics, and a good start is all about position, energy flow, and simultaneously holding yourself posed and ready *and* relaxed.

Get your sitting position, your hand position, and your fingering right, and good technique will follow.

# Posture and Position

## In This Chapter

- Determining the correct sitting position
- Developing a good hand position
- Finding finger numbers and finger placement
- Using the whole body
- Avoiding injuries from tension and overuse

Playing piano seems to be something you do with only your fingers. In reality, a pianist uses wrist muscles, arm muscles, and shoulder muscles. As with so many other physical activities—from ballet to kayaking to golf to yoga—the pianist's energy comes from the central core of the body. How we sit determines how we access this energy. How we hold our hands determines how we transfer this energy to the keyboard. How we move our fingers determines how smoothly we play.

Of course, all of that is easier said than done. Is the chair height correct? Are you sitting straight? Are your arms the right distance from the fallboard? Are your hands cupped in the right shape? At first, playing the piano in the correct position can seem somewhat like taking a golf lesson: in both cases, instructors demand that you do seemingly impossible and contradictory things all at the same time— and relax while you're at it. But with time, the correct position becomes second nature.

# How to Sit

A comfortable, ergonomic piano-playing position starts with sitting. But as it turns out, sitting is more complicated than it may first appear.

The correct position for playing the piano takes into account the pianist's height, torso size, and arm length, and involves adjusting the height of the chair or bench and its distance from the piano.

## Piano Bench Height

The first issue is the height of the piano bench. A good piano bench should be adjustable (this rules out most of the matching wooden benches that are sold with pianos). Adjustable benches can be expensive artist benches (which can run $500 and up) or far less expensive metal and vinyl benches sold at stores that carry digital pianos (which run at a much more affordable $50 and up).

Pianists differ not only in terms of their overall height and size, but also according to whether they have long legs and short torsos or short legs and long torsos (or some other combination). Contrary to what seems intuitive, the height of the piano bench does not exactly correlate to the height of the pianist.

Instead, the bench should be adjusted so that when the pianist puts his fingertips on the keys, his forearms more or less lay flat (parallel with the floor). For tall people (especially those with long torsos), this position generally requires setting the bench's height at its lowest setting. Smaller adults and children need to sit higher.

Unfortunately, the piano is a one-size-fits-all kind of instrument. The same instrument is used for a 6-foot, 6-inch basketball player and a 5-foot-nothing ballerina. In general, taller people sit much lower than do shorter people, but this means that the tall person has to somehow fold his or her legs under the piano.

## Sitting Position

"Sit up straight" is some generic parenting advice that pianists would do well to obey. There's a reason piano benches don't come with seatbacks: if a pianist were to lean against a chair's back, her arms would be in a position that makes it virtually impossible to play. The hands wouldn't be able sink properly into the keybeds, and the arm weight would be misdirected.

Instead, pianists should sit up straight and slightly forward on the bench. The distance between the chair and the piano should be adjusted so that when the pianist loosely reaches her hands forward, she can rap her knuckles against the piano's fallboard. The feet should be planted squarely on the floor, near the pedals.

*Sitting at the piano.*

### Making Adjustments for Children

Small children are dwarfed by standard-size pianos, and the resulting discomfort has an impact on their technique. There are two solutions to this problem: make some adjustments or use a keyboard.

Digital keyboards (assuming that they have properly weighted keys with touch control) can be perfectly acceptable starter instruments for children. Some teachers prefer to use keyboards with very young students because the keyboards can be placed on adjustable stands closer to the floor, meaning that a child can put his feet on the floor and reach the pedals. Keyboards also tend to have a lighter action than an acoustic piano, which may be easier for small children to handle.

On a standard acoustic piano, a foot block can be used so that the child's feet don't dangle. This helps the child feel grounded. For children who are ready to use the pedals before they are quite large enough to reach them, foot blocks with pedal extenders are available.

# Hand Position

Correct hand position is one of the most essential issues in developing good technique. So when beginning each of the exercises in this book, the first step should be checking to be sure your hand position is correct.

**THEORY AND PRACTICE**

Correct hand position is not a one-size-fits-all issue. It varies because pianists' hands vary. The great twentieth-century pianist Vladimir Horowitz was famously known for playing with flat fingers—the kind of hand position that piano teachers flatly declare to be unacceptable. Yet Horowitz was able to play flawless, lightning-fast runs. Indeed, this same flat-fingered position is favored by some jazz artists, many of whom did not have formal lessons, and still seem to fly across the piano at the speed of light.

While it is true that some great pianists play using an idiosyncratic hand position, the fact remains that, for most of the rest of us, the standard round-hand position described in the next section provides more control, dexterity, and speed. The challenge is that this position does not feel at all natural to the beginning piano student. It may not even feel comfortable to a piano student who has had many years of lessons without much attention to technique. Some students are lucky enough to have a naturally good hand position, while others need constant reinforcement from teachers. Unfortunately, this aspect of playing the piano is sometimes ignored.

The results are evident when students try to tackle more advanced music. Many piano teachers have had the experience of trying to coach a returning adult student who has somehow managed to learn the notes to a popular, virtuosic war-horse of the classical repertoire. Yet although the notes are learned, students with poor technique can't ever quite manage to get these pieces under their fingers. Lack of a good hand position means they lack the necessary control.

### Finding the Correct Hand Position

It's time to go to the keyboard and practice finding and moving your fingers in the correct hand position.

To start, place the four fingers (all but the thumb) on a flat surface so that the fingertips are lined up in a fairly straight line.

Now lift your hand, and, without moving any of those four fingers, make an "O" by touching the tip of your thumb to the tip of your index finger.

Next, take your hand (in this position) to the piano and let the fingers relax just a little, enough so that each finger is on one white key. (Tell yourself "One key per finger, one finger per key.")

Make sure that the side of the thumb, near the first joint, is making contact with the piano key, and that the knuckles are raised and rounded (as they were when you made the "O"). It's almost as though you are gently holding something round in your palm. Your wrists should be loosely flexed, at keyboard height.

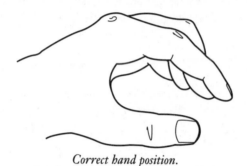

*Correct hand position.*

Now practice pressing down different fingers, trying to keep the other fingers and the rest of your hand fairly quiet and still. If your fingers are properly rounded, you should feel that you are using the muscles under your knuckles to raise and lower the fingers.

## This Little Piggy Went to Market ...

For the pianist, fingers are numbered starting with the thumb of both hands being number one. The index finger is number two, the middle finger is number three, the ring finger is number four, and the pinky is number five.

If you played a different instrument at one time, such as guitar, you may be used to different finger numbers. In piano, we count the thumb, and we count outward on both hands. This is universal.

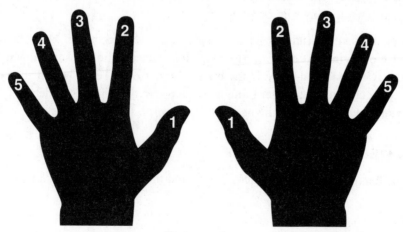

*Finger numbers.*

In Chapter 3, we discuss the importance of correct fingerings. For now, just note that in piano books—including this one—fingers are numbered from the thumbs out, from one to five.

## Finger Placement on the Keys

In this book, we start with white key exercises, and then move on to exercises that include black keys. But it should be noted that most music involves both white keys and black keys. Therefore, the fingers should be positioned on the keys so that both white keys and black keys are reachable without excessive movement back and forth.

This means that the fingertips usually sit on the white keys about a third of the way in, near the end of the black keys. Of course, finger placement greatly depends on which finger and which playing position. Frequently, the thumb and the pinky will find themselves, out of necessity, sitting on the edge of a white key. And when playing a piece with many black notes, the fingers playing white notes may slide farther in between the black notes. But as a starting position, keep the fingertips of the second, third, and fourth fingers on the white keys about a third of the way in.

## Nail Length

To play the piano, nails have to be short, which means that they must not extend beyond the top of the finger. (Shorter is even better.)

Pianists typically play on the pad of each finger, just beneath the nail. If nails are too long, however, the pianist is forced to play with flat fingers, which is disastrous for learning good piano technique. Long nails can catch in between the keys (and tear off); they also click and slide. Quite simply, this is one of those sacrifices a pianist has to make for her art.

Adult women and teenage girls are sometimes resistant to the idea that they cannot play piano with long nails. But this is one of those bottom-line rules that is impossible to circumvent. You can't run the Olympic 100-meter race in high heels, you can't play volleyball in an evening gown, and you can't play the piano with long nails.

## Starting Exercises for Finger Position

Now that you have your hands rounded, your wrists low (but not sagging), your nails cut, and your fingers on the keys, let's try some exercises.

In the following exercises, remember that each finger stays on one note and plays that note. We'll move out of this position quickly enough, but for now, staying in one place will make things a bit easier and allow you to concentrate on the feel and sound of the piano.

Play the following five-finger pattern (we repeat this pattern quite a bit in the next couple of chapters). The exercise is written out for both hands. Start by playing with just the right hand, then just the left hand, then both hands together.

Now try playing the exercise different ways:

- Like you're angry

- Like you're lulling a baby to sleep

- Like you're touching a hot stove

- Like you want to disturb the neighbors who had a loud party last night

- As fast as you can

- Starting quietly and getting louder

- Starting loudly and fading away

**FLYING FINGERS**

As you play, try to keep your fingers and hands still. Each finger should lift and press independently; don't use the big muscles of the wrist to "help out." Be sure to keep the same fingers on their respective notes (as noted in the first measure and throughout the exercise), and don't let your hand slip.

# The Rest of the Body

It's interesting to note how much the *piano* has changed since Bartolomeo Christofori invented (or at least popularized) the earliest *pianofortes* starting in the early 1700s. Cristofori's piano was a delicate instrument, more like a harpsichord than like today's enormous and powerful concert grand piano.

The earliest pianists were taught to sit very still. The keys had an easy, light action, so arm weight was not necessary to push them down. Indeed, a full-blown fortissimo attack such as that used today on, say, a Rachmaninoff concerto, would have undoubtedly broken strings, and maybe even the frames, of these frail instruments.

**UNIVERSAL LANGUAGE**

**Piano** means "softly" in Italian. Why is the biggest, loudest instrument—one that can hold its own against an entire orchestra in a piano concerto—called "the quiet"? Early pianos were the first keyboard instruments with which volume could be controlled by the touch of the fingers on the keys. This ability was so new and important that the piano was named for what it could do: play softly and loudly. Hence, the instrument was named the **pianoforte** (or *fortepiano*). Laziness and abbreviation resulted in this grand instrument being called "the quiet."

Today's pianist plays bigger pieces on a much larger and stronger instrument. As a result, pianists need to use a varied range of techniques, depending on the type of music being played and the desired effect. Clearly, one plays a Scarlatti Sonata far differently than a Chopin Polonaise or twentieth-century honky-tonk blues. In the first instance, the pianist might well sit very quietly. In the second case, arms may move freely and forcefully to achieve the strength and speed needed to perform certain technical feats. But in all cases, the use of today's grand piano requires more than more finger weight. Arms and shoulder muscles can also be involved, although less for Bach than for Brahms.

Serious students need to remember that playing the piano is an athletic undertaking. The major concert works require enormous finger, wrist, and forearm strength, as well as skill, dexterity, coordination, and endurance. Just like a casual weekend runner who used to be a competitive marathoner can't suddenly decide to run a marathon and expect to equal his champion time, the casual pianist who used to play Chopin's "Heroic Polonaise" probably can't survive the double-octaves section if he practices only an hour or two a week.

## Preventing Injury

It is unlikely that a person with no unusual physical challenges would injure himself practicing piano half an hour a day, no matter how intensely. Serious pianists who practice several hours a day, on the other hand, are at risk for certain injuries. Over time, overuse and stress injuries can develop, particularly for people who may have a pre-existing susceptibility (for example, someone who already types for several hours a day may be at risk for *carpal tunnel syndrome*, which can also occur with piano playing).

**UNIVERSAL LANGUAGE**

**Carpal tunnel syndrome** is an injury to the wrists caused by inflammation of the tissue surrounding the nerves. Pianists who already spend long hours doing repetitive motions such as typing may be at more risk of developing carpal tunnel syndrome. If you feel pain in your wrists, stop what you are doing. Shake out your hands and vary the practice routine, perhaps by switching hands or turning to a different exercise.

To avoid injury:

- Vary which practice tasks you do.

- If something hurts, stop doing it. Change hands, change pieces, change the element being practiced, and/or take a break.

- Shake out your hands, trying to make them as much like a rag doll as possible.

- Try not to be tense. This is easier said than done for many adult students.

Relaxation and stretching exercises can include yoga, Alexander technique, or simply taking several deep breaths.

# How to Practice

The exercises in this book are designed to develop the strength and dexterity necessary to approach beginning, intermediate, and even some advanced work of the piano, jazz, and popular repertoires. But as with any athletic endeavor, they must be practiced on a regular basis, or muscles soon grow flabby and reluctant.

How much is enough? The short answer: no amount of practice is ever enough, because there is always more to learn. But given that most of us can't devote our working lives to piano, half an hour to an hour most days yields noticeable and fulfilling progress for the adult student. You won't get to Carnegie Hall on that (unless you buy a ticket, of course), but you might make it to your local open-mic night.

Begin each practice session with a few minutes of warm-ups taken from this book. Don't try to work through it all at once—this book has enough exercises in it for years of practicing. Indeed, after 40 years of playing the piano, I still do some of these drills.

Try to play all exercises in time. That means playing with a metronome (as described in Chapter 13), counting, tapping your foot, or snapping the fingers of your free hand—anything to create the feeling of a steady rhythmic pulse. Music is always played in rhythm; exercises should be, too.

## The Least You Need to Know

- Sitting correctly at the piano enables pianists to access their energy ergonomically and improves playing technique.
- Correct hand position is not intuitive, but it is essential to being able to play difficult technical passages.
- Correct technique may require you to use finger weight, arm weight, and shoulder muscles, depending on the style of music and the desired sound.
- Relaxation exercises, taking breaks, and switching practice tasks helps the pianist avoid injuries.

# Basic Fingering

## In This Chapter

- The importance of fingerings
- Basic fingering principles
- How fingerings help pianists reach musical and expressive goals
- Choosing fingerings to suit both the hand and the music

Fingering—knowing which finger to put on which note, under what circumstances, and in which sequence—is one of the most important elements of developing good piano technique. To see why, let's go back to the golf example. A golfer learns a sequence of exact and precise motions, starting with positioning the body, then raising the club, then balancing and controlling the placement and movement of body weight, and finally following through with a swing that travels in a prescribed arc. He then repeats that exact series of movements, time after time.

The golfer doesn't sometimes grab the club with one hand on top and the other in a different place. As much as possible, he tries to repeat the same exact pattern of movements. Certainly, as our golfer becomes more skilled, he will develop multiple swing patterns for each club or to send the ball different distances. But the golfer's control is all based on having practiced the same series of motions. Having repeated the same exact motions an uncountable number of times gives his brain a repertoire of patterns to use and reuse in new contexts.

The same is true of piano: fingering is a sequence of practiced physical moves that allows us to play with intention and control.

## Fingering: Why Care?

I cannot overstate the importance of correct fingering. Beginning and intermediate students must use consistent fingering to train the brain. Advanced pianists do not play one note at a time, any more than a literate person reads a book one letter at a time. Consistent fingering is required to play notes in a fluid sequence.

At the same time, it is important to understand that there are often several possible fingerings for a passage, and that part of the pianist's bag of tools is the ability to determine which set of fingerings will work best for her particular hand shape and technique.

**SOUR NOTES**

A word of warning for beginners, whose music reading skills are still shaky: finger numbers are not a substitute for reading notes! Starting in a typical five-finger position, many students get used to the fact that the thumb plays the first note, the second finger plays the second note, and so on. While that may work for five-finger nursery rhymes, it stops working as soon as the music becomes more complex. After all, the piano has 88 keys, and the pianist has only 10 fingers.

Finger numbers tell you which finger to put on a note, but they don't help you identify the note: that's what note reading is for. Falling into the habit of assuming that finger numbers can be a substitute for notes not only delays learning to read music, but also ensures playing lots of wrong notes in the meantime.

Indeed, different editions of the same piece of music may have very different fingerings according to the editor's way of thinking. If you happen to have multiple editions of the same work on hand, go ahead and see which fingering seems to suit you better. But unless you have a teacher to check with, stick with the suggested fingerings, except for those that are completely impossible (for example, your fingers can't make a particular reach). Most beginning and intermediate pianists haven't yet learned how to choose fingerings that work ergonomically, fit into the entire phrase, support the musical intent of the composer, and work in repeated similar phrases.

As with hand position, some students take to fingering more naturally than others. Students, especially young children, often quite naturally put their hands in positions and use their fingers in sequences that would never occur to a trained pianist.

The biggest fingering mistake beginning students (and many intermediates) make is that they are concerned only with getting from the note they are currently playing to the next correct note. As a result, they use whichever finger seems handiest to get to that next note. Unfortunately, their choice doesn't consider where they are going next.

**FLYING FINGERS**

If a published fingering doesn't make sense at first, ask yourself what the editor may have been thinking. To set up the correct position for a run that has a gnarly sequence of notes a measure ahead, the editor may choose a fingering that looks awkward at first—but that makes it possible to play the difficult section coming up. Always remember that good fingering is not merely a matter of getting from one place to the next, but also of being in a position to continue on in the music.

Good fingering is not only concerned with what notes you play, but also how you play them. Although beginning and intermediate students are often unaware of this, correct fingering helps the pianist play the notes with the correct articulation, dynamics, and phrasing. In other words, fingering is not only a technical issue, but also a musical one. Different fingerings do indeed have an effect on how a pianist connects, articulates, phrases, and voices the various notes in a passage.

So fingering facilitates the pianist's ability to technically perform a piece, solidly learn it, and realize its musical meaning. No wonder it is one of the most important aspects of learning to play the piano.

**SOUR NOTES**

It takes enormous discipline, but don't try to learn a piece and think that you can fix the fingering later. In their eagerness to get started, many students skim over the fingering—which means learning an incorrect fingering that needs later adjustment. The earlier you learn the correct fingering, the more solidly you will retain it. Correct fingering is as much a part of the music as correct notes, rhythm, and phrasing. Indeed, correct notes, rhythm, and phrasing may be impossible without the correct fingers.

# The Ergonomics of Fingering

The "obvious" fingering is not always the optimal one.

Let's start with a basic five-finger position used by virtually every beginning piano student: one finger per note, one note per finger.

You probably noticed that those last five notes were a little tricky to play (and if you tried to play them quickly, or quickly and loudly, they'd be even more difficult). Some fingers are stronger than others, and trilling (going back and forth between two notes; see Chapter 22) with the fourth fingers is difficult. Even highly skilled pianists try to avoid it when possible—and an altered fingering makes avoiding it possible.

Changing the fingering requires a little planning and looking at the phrase as a whole. Instead of playing one note per finger and one finger per note, try putting your thumb on the D at the end of the second measure, and then stretching up to put the third finger on the G. This may seem ungainly at first, but after you've learned it, you'll probably find that it's much easier to play those Gs and Fs quickly with stronger fingers.

It's true that this fingering takes a bit of thinking. It also takes practice to learn how to contract fingers (which we discuss in Chapter 6). But it also turns out that this fingering is much easier than trilling quickly and fluently with the pinky.

If we then move the exercise into the key of F, the problem of the weak fourth and fifth fingers becomes even more awkward—and the solution of switching fingers becomes more attractive because of the Bb. In the following example, the first two measures are fingered the first way; the second two measures are fingered the second way. Notice how much easier it is to play the second two measures. The last five notes are much easier to play with the second and third fingers than with the fourth and fifth fingers.

So the obvious fingering is not always the right one. Fingering needs to be considered within the context of the entire phrase. In Chapters 6 and 17, we look at different fingering challenges and how to solve them.

# Role of the Individual's Hand

All of this talk about standard fingerings and correct fingerings has to take into account the most important variable of all: individual variations. Hand size, stretch, and strength all affect fingering choices on an individual level. Some fingerings suggested by an editor or a composer may be impossible for a pianist who can't reach a particular interval. Sometimes, editors give choices.

And of course, hand and finger strength issues also come into play. Many beginning and intermediate students favor their stronger fingers. In particular, students tend to avoid the weaker fourth finger. These fingering habits need to be corrected as early as possible so that the student doesn't fall into the unconscious habit of never using a particular finger. Similarly, fingerings may feel initially awkward to beginning and intermediate students, but this is not a reason to avoid pursuing them. What feels awkward today may, with practice, become easy and useful.

**THEORY AND PRACTICE**

The weak fourth finger has plagued pianists for centuries. The great composer Robert Schumann suffered permanent injury to his right hand; the injury is thought to have been caused by his use of a mechanical contraption meant to strengthen his fourth finger. Whether or not the contraption was the cause of the injury, the fact remains that the pesky, weak ring finger has frustrated even the greatest pianists.

Advanced players often use alternate fingerings, which they have learned work for their particular hands. But these are based on years of practicing standard fingerings and alternatives, so they develop a hand-sense of how to choose fingerings. More advanced fingering techniques are discussed in detail in Chapter 16; for now, it is important to remember the following:

- Do not refinger scales, arpeggios, and basic cadences.

- Try the recommended fingering several times before refingering. Often, it takes a few readings to absorb what the editor is suggesting.

- Be aware that a fingering that seems comfortable and playable at a slow learning tempo may not work at a fast performance tempo. Solicit the advice of a teacher who can tell you whether the proposed fingering can work at the performance tempo.

- Realize that sometimes fingerings that seem odd or idiosyncratic have a musical motivation to help achieve a musical goal.

- Above all, once you decide on a fingering, stick with it!

## The Least You Need to Know

- There may be several acceptable fingerings for many passages of music.
- Seemingly awkward fingerings may have a musical or ergonomic purpose that is not immediately obvious.
- Fingerings are concerned with getting through an entire series of notes—not just getting from one note to another.
- Fingerings should be consistent.

# Starting to Move

## In This Chapter

- Two-finger warm-up exercises
- Three-finger warm-up exercises
- Five-finger warm-up exercises
- Hands together warm-up exercises

In Chapters 1 and 2, you learned about the importance of good hand position and fingering. In this chapter, you'll start to play basic exercises to develop finger strength and dexterity, and to apply good hand position to the keyboard.

This chapter contains basic dexterity exercises appropriate for elementary students who have learned to read music. The exercises in this chapter are designed to help students become familiar with the keyboard, move around from position to position, and exercise different finger combinations. These starting exercises stay in simple positions, allowing easy moves on the keyboard. You also stay on the white notes throughout this chapter, so that you can concentrate on finger movement and position without worrying about sharps and flats.

## Practice Tips for Warm-Up Exercises

Throughout all of the exercises in this chapter—and indeed, throughout the whole book—always start by making sure that your hands are in the correct position. For running passages, the fingers should always be curved, the hands rounded, and the wrists relaxed and low (although not below the level of the keys). Check before you play!

Next, be sure that all fingering choices are deliberate. The fingerings given in this book for scales, arpeggios, and other exercises are the standard fingerings used today, and they are a good place to start.

Exercises should be played in strict time. (See Chapter 13 for tips on playing with a metronome.) Start slowly, and then try edging up to a faster tempo. When playing with one hand, you can also tap or keep time with the other hand. This helps you to internalize the beat.

Look at the music, not at your hands! These exercises provide the core base of musical material you will find in pieces from Baroque to blues, and being able to play them without looking will yield big dividends down the road. In playing real music, there are many instances in which you will have to quickly glance down at your hands to ensure that a big leap lands on the right note, or that a difficult transition is managed correctly. But only glance at your hands; as a pianist, your gaze should primarily rest on the music. When practicing, notice that your peripheral vision gives you a lot of information about your hand placement.

**THEORY AND PRACTICE**

Keep in mind that when you encounter scales and arpeggios in actual music, what comes before, what comes after, and what is added in the middle may well require you to use a different fingering. The standard fingerings you are learning in this book give you a base of knowledge, and a place from which to start. But composers write music, not exercises—frequently, you will have to make fingering choices and changes that you should write into the music so you can remember and stick with them (assuming they work). Above all, be consistent.

When you have learned an exercise or a pattern, play it with your eyes closed to absorb the feel of the mechanical motion. Knowing you can play a passage with your eyes closed gives you an enormous amount of confidence, especially when the exercise requires position changes.

**FLYING FINGERS**

As you are playing these exercises, keep these things in mind:

- The exercises in this chapter are short. Learn them one at a time, and practice them until you can play them fluently, without missing a beat or stopping to find a note.
- The easier, shorter exercises can be played with the eyes closed.
- Once fluency has been achieved, play each exercise five times in a row.
- Be sure to stress the beat and rhythm (as demonstrated in the recorded examples).

# Two-Finger Warm-Ups

Practice the following right-hand warm-up exercise. As you did in Chapter 2, after you've learned the pattern, try varying the touch: loud, soft, staccato, and so on. Practice each exercise five or six times.

The following exercises help develop finger strength of fingers next to each other. Try to keep your hand still; the muscles of the fingers and knuckle should be doing the work. Start by working the fingers of the right hand.

 **Track 1a, Example 1**

Now it's time to move on to the left hand.

**Track 1b (0:24), Example 2**

## Warm-Ups for Skipping Fingers

The following exercises involve skipping from space notes to space notes or line notes to line notes. For beginning music readers, learning these intervals, which are called "thirds," is a big help in music reading.

Now it's the left hand's turn.

# The Slur

The following exercises introduce a musical idea known as the slur, in which the hand lowers to drop into the first note, then slightly raises for the second note. The slur is found frequently in classical music, and it is a subtle yet powerful expressive device. The exercises should first be played with the first and second fingers (as shown in the next figure), first with the right hand, and then with the left hand. You can also try these exercises with different fingerings to see how they feel.

Start practicing the slur by using the first and second fingers.

**Track 2a, Example 3**

Slurs are less frequently played with the left hand, but you'll develop dexterity by practicing them.

 **Track 2b (0:26), Example 4**

Slurs should also be practiced with the third and fourth fingers. Again, start with the right hand, then continue with the left hand.

**Track 2c (0:48), Example 5**

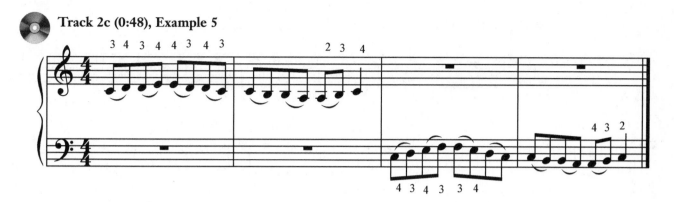

Finally, practice the slur with fingers four and five. This will undoubtedly feel a little awkward, but it's an important skill, especially for the right hand.

**Track 2d (1:03), Example 6**

# Three-Finger Warm-Ups (Hands Separate)

In the following exercises, the first line uses fingers one, two, and three; the second line uses fingers two, three, and four; and the third line uses fingers three, four, and five. Start by playing the exercises with the right hand.

The same pattern is repeated in the left-hand version.

## Five-Finger Warm-Ups

In the following exercises, all five fingers are used in the same sequence. You'll notice that only the starting finger is given. By this point, you should be familiar enough with the five-finger position to play the correct notes with the correct fingers simply by keeping your hand still and playing the fingers in sequence. Leaving out the finger numbers also will help you avoid the temptation to cheat with note reading by looking at numbers instead of notes. Try to play these lines of music in strict time.

Start by practicing the five-finger right-hand warm-ups.

Now practice the left-hand warm-ups.

## Moving Up and Down the Keyboard

The following exercise is based on a simple pattern. Start by learning to play the first two measures. Then move your hands up to the next position, as shown in the music, and continue playing the pattern up the keyboard. Notice, as you do so, how it sounds different when started on different notes. Start with the right hand.

Now it's time for the left hand. Try to be sure that your left hand sounds as fluent as your right hand. (This can be difficult for right-handed people.)

# Hands Together

Once you have mastered the foregoing exercises, it's time to put your hands together.

The first example exercise is in contrary motion. The hands are mirror images of each other and the same fingers are always playing at the same time.

The second example is in parallel motion, in which the hands play the same notes. This is a little trickier, because it involves each hand playing with different fingers.

In the final exercise in this chapter, you'll play completely different things with your right and left hands. The right hand will start by playing the tune, with a left-hand ostinato (accompaniment pattern). Then the left hand will take the tune, and the right hand will play the accompaniment. See if you can bring out the tune by playing first the right hand a little louder, and then the left hand a little louder.

 **Track 3, Example 7**

## The Least You Need to Know

- All exercises should be played with rounded fingers.
- Practice with one hand at a time.
- Choose a steady tempo; you can always go faster later.
- Keep your eyes on the music, not on your fingers.

# Moving Along

Your first task: learn how to control your fingers. Start in a basic five-finger position so you just have to worry about one thing at a time. Then you'll learn to move around to other five-finger positions to become familiar with all 12 keys (oh yeah, and the 12 minor keys, too).

Don't stop there! Next up is learning to move around the keyboard using standard techniques, such as crossing your fingers over each other and stretching to a new position. Then I put you to work playing several notes at once and practicing exercises that help you develop fluency in making and using chords and chord patterns. Get your tip jar ready for when you take these skills on the road.

# Major Pentascales and Chords

## In This Chapter

- Making major pentascales
- Making major chords
- Practicing major five-finger patterns
- Using major pentascales and chords to improvise

In this chapter, we look at five-note scales, sometimes called pentascales. Remember the "Do Re Mi" song from *The Sound of Music*? The five-note major pentascale is simply the first five notes of this scale: Do, Re, Mi, Fa, Sol.

Why stop there? Simply because the pianist has five fingers and the pentascale has five notes. Learning how to move comfortably around the first five notes of all the scales in a simple five-finger position helps you learn to control each finger without having to also worry about moving all over the keyboard.

The pentascales help you to get familiar with the first five notes of all 12 scales (one for each black and white note), and get your fingers moving in a good basic position, using both black and white notes.

## Finding the Major Pentascales

Each of the 12 pentascales has its own unique combination of black and white notes. But it isn't necessary to memorize them to learn them, because all 12 of the pentascales use the same exact pattern. Understanding how they are made will enable you to find any of the 12 scales. You don't have to remember all the notes of all the scales; you simply have to remember how to find them.

The starting note of the pentascale is the key in which you are playing. For example, the C pentascale starts on C, and the C♯ pentascale starts on C♯. The notes in a scale are either a half step apart from each other (from one note to the very next note) or a whole step apart from each other (two half steps). Each key has its own combination of white notes and black notes; when you are playing in a key, you are using those notes most of the time, and you end on that note, which gives your piece a sense of finality and resolution.

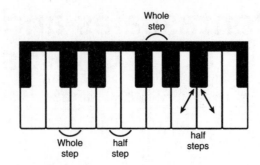

Let's start on C and apply the following pattern:

> The starting note is C
>
> Go up a whole step (D)
>
> Go up a whole step (E)
>
> Go up a half step (F)
>
> Go up a whole step (G)

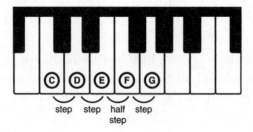

Because the piano is so visual, with black and white notes laid out, these patterns of whole steps and half steps are easy to see and identify.

We are also going to use the pentascale to find the chord that goes with the first note of the scale. In the key of C, the C chord contains the notes C, E, and G. Notice that these are the first, third, and fifth notes of the pattern. Once you have learned the five-finger pentascale pattern, you can find any major chord on the piano.

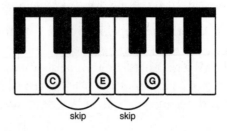

You'll probably notice that the following pattern feels familiar. That's because many of the exercises you learned in Chapter 3 worked with the notes of the C Major pentascale.

After you have gotten used to this position, it is time to play around with it a little. You've already played quite a few exercises in the C Major pentascale, so in this chapter, we move into other positions that use sharps and flats.

# Examples in Other Five-Finger Positions

A pentascale can be built on any note. Each pentascale contains five notes organized by step and skips. All of them sound like the first five notes of a Do-Re-Mi scale.

Let's look at the D pentascale as an example:

> The starting note is D
>
> Go up a whole step (E)
>
> Go up a whole step (F♯)
>
> Go up a half step (G)
>
> Go up a whole step (A)

All 12 pentascales are written out. Notice the *key signatures* at the start of each new pentascale. In scales in which there are many black notes, be sure that your fingers are positioned correctly on the keys: not at the edge of the white keys, but rather close to the ends of the black keys, or even in between them a little (as discussed in Chapter 1). Be sure your fingers are curved in the correct position. It is awkward to try to play black and white key patterns with flat fingers.

**UNIVERSAL LANGUAGE**

**Key signatures** are the group of sharps and/or flats at the beginning of each line of music. They tell you how many sharps and/or flats the piece has and which ones they are. If there is an F♯ at the beginning of a line of music, this tells you that every F in the whole song is an F♯, unless the composer marks it with a natural sign (♮). Each key has its own group of sharps or flats, so knowing the key signature helps you figure out which key the piece of music is in.

After you have gotten comfortable playing these scales, feel free to noodle around and make up little tunes just to get used to moving around in them. You should also practice finding these pentascales quickly, starting on any note. Use the whole-step and half-step pattern to find the notes.

*continues*

*continued*

# Transposing Using Pentascales

Transposing is the ability to play a piece of music in a different key than the key it is written in. While solo classical pianists rarely need to transpose, transposing is an essential skill for almost everyone else. Accompanists transpose frequently, especially when playing with singers, who may not be physically able to sing a song in its original key. Keyboard players who work with horn players find themselves transposing because wind players are much more comfortable in flat keys due to how their instruments produce sound.

In this book, many of the exercises are presented in one key, but once each exercise is mastered, you should practice it in different keys. The transposing exercises in this chapter will help you get started in learning this important skill.

While most songs use far more than five notes, knowing how to transpose using the basic pentascale gives pianists a foundation for more complex transposing.

Let's try this with the well-known song "When the Saints Go Marching In." In the following example, notice that I've included both the notes in the key of C and the finger numbers you would use in a five-finger C position:

Now let's move "When the Saints Go Marching In" over to the D Major pentascale. To do this, first find the D Major pentascale.

Now we are going to play the same sequence of notes as we did when we played the song in C, but instead of the first finger playing C, it will play D. Finger number two is now on E, finger three is on F♯, four is on G, and five is on A.

Now let's try it in A♭. Again, first find the pentascale:

Then play the notes in the correct order of the song.

Go ahead and try to transpose "When the Saints Go Marching In" into all 12 keys.

 **THEORY AND PRACTICE**

There are several ways to think about transposing, and most good pianists use all of them at various times.

- Finger numbers: In these simple pieces, move hand position and play the same finger numbers in a different scale. While this is a good way to get started, simply knowing the fingers isn't enough in more complex music pieces.

- Steps and skips: Reading the intervals, or distances between the notes in the piece, is an effective way to transpose. For example, if the piece starts by going up by a full step from C to D, in the key of E, it would also start with a full step, from E to F♯.

- Transposition interval: If the piece is transposed up by a full step (the interval is called a "second"), then every note in the new key will be a full step (a second) higher than every note in the original key.

- Harmonies: Advanced pianists also look at the harmonies, but this requires knowledge of music theory.

- Playing by ear: Pianists differ as to how accurately their ears can guide them. If you know how the original song goes, you may be able to accurately pick it out in the new key simply by imagining the sounds.

# Pentascale Exercises in All 12 Positions

The following exercises require the fingers to move in different sequences. First, learn them as written, in the key of C. Once you are comfortable playing them, try moving them around to different keys.

Notice that each exercise begins with playing the notes of the five-finger position in order, followed by the chord. This is to help you when you transpose, by reintroducing you to the new position. Remember to tell yourself the name of the chord as you play it. This doubles the benefits of the exercise: not only are you learning the positions and working your fingers, but you also are learning to understand what you are doing so you can later apply it in different contexts.

Beginners should learn the patterns in two-measure phrases. More advanced students can learn four measures at a time, or even the full eight-measure pattern. Once you can play the patterns fluently, start transposing them into all 12 different pentascales. If you need help, refer to the sheet music showing all the pentascales in all keys earlier in this chapter.

It should be noted that different pianists take to transposing at very different rates, depending on their previous training, skill level, ear, and aptitude for this skill. It can take several weeks—or even longer—to get the hang of it, so don't rush the process. Introduce your fingers to one new pentascale a day, or even every few days. There's no particular value in learning this fast.

**Track 4a, Example 1**

## Two Hands at a Time

If you are like most people, you have favored your dominant hand when playing the exercises. Go back and be sure that, if you are right-handed, you haven't neglected your left hand. (And the reverse for you southpaws.) Now you're going to put two hands together, as you did in Chapter 2—only this time, once you've learned the piece, you're going to transpose it into all 12 keys.

**Track 4b (0:38), Example 2**

As with the previous exercise, if necessary, break the study up into two-measure segments, and practice until you can play it fluently. Only after you have learned the piece should you start to transpose.

## Improvisation Exercise for Pentascales

Now that you've learned to play the pentascales in different keys, let's move on to playing a sequence of scales. In the following exercises, the left hand will move from chord to chord, and the right hand should "noodle round" by playing random notes in the corresponding position. First, listen to the recorded track while following the chord changes written out here.

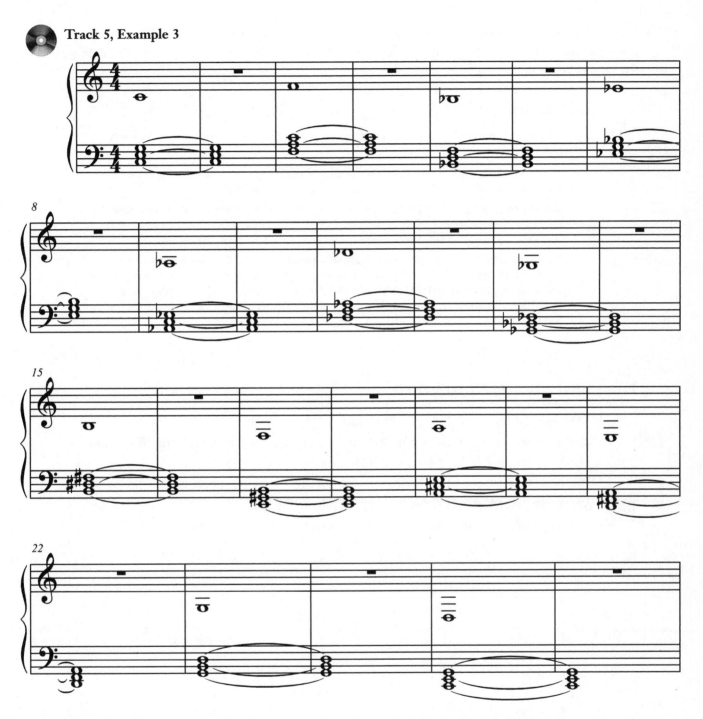

**Track 5, Example 3**

Now it's time to play. After listening to the recorded example, you'll hear four clicks, then some left-hand chords. To improvise over these, simply use the notes in the pentascales (the starting note for each pentascale is given). You are not expected to try to copy the example on the recording. It's just there to show you what can be done using the pentascales over their related chords. Notice that the improvisation is played in strict rhythm, meaning that the improvisation only takes as long as the allotted beats for that chord.

Notice also that each chord gets eight beats for your improvisation (two measures). The sheet music gives you only the chord for the left hand and the starting note for the right hand. What you do with the other beats is up to you! So have fun with it.

**FLYING FINGERS**

Learning to improvise can be daunting. Here are some tips to perhaps make the process a little less intimidating:

- Don't be afraid of wrong notes. If you play a note that sounds simply awful against a chord, quickly pass over to the next note, which is guaranteed to sound good.

- The notes that will sound most consonant with your chord are the notes that are actually in that chord, so those are the notes you should play on the stronger beats of each measure (especially the first beat). Save the other notes to play in between; these are called passing tones.

- Be sure to play everything in time. If in doubt, set a metronome at 100 beats per minute, and try to play along with the clicks. If you are working with an electronic keyboard, it can also be fun to add a drum track and play along with that. Always remember: music takes place in time. Everything else—notes, technique, phrasing, and dynamics—is subservient to the fact that music must move smoothly and regularly through time, at a steady beat.

## The Least You Need to Know

- The major pentascales are the first five notes of the Do-Re-Mi scale.
- Practicing pentascales and patterns using them allows you to familiarize yourself with moving your fingers in different positions and keys.
- The major chord in any key is made up of the first, third, and fifth notes of the pentascale.
- Transposing means moving a tune or pattern into a different key.
- Matching scales to their related chords is the basis for beginning improvisation.

# Minor Pentascales and Chords

## In This Chapter

- Making minor pentascales
- Making minor chords
- Practicing minor five-finger patterns
- Using minor pentascales and chords to improvise

You may not know the musical theory associated with making a minor scale, but you undoubtedly know what they are; just think of the sound of a funeral march.

Songs and pieces written in minor keys are often described as sounding darker, sadder, or more somber. As with major pentascales, minor pentascales are simply the first five notes of any minor scale. Learning these patterns solidifies an understanding of how to make minor chords, and gives the fingers practice in finding and moving from major to minor patterns.

## Finding the Minor Pentascales

As with major pentascales, each of the 12 different notes in the chromatic scales has its own combination of notes that form a minor pentascale. If you've mastered the major pentascales in Chapter 4, the minor scales will be a snap. The only difference is that the third note of the minor pentascale is a half-step lower than the third note of the major pentascale.

For example, in the key of C, the major pentascale contains the notes C, D, E, F, and G.

**Track 6a, Example 1**

The C minor pentascale contains C, D, E♭, F, and G. The only difference is that instead of an E in the middle, we have an E♭.

**Track 6b (0:08), Example 2**

Notice what a difference that one single note makes in sound!

As with major pentascales, each minor key has a key signature that tells us right at the beginning of the line how many sharps or flats we need to play, and which ones they are. The key of C minor is written correctly with three flats right at the beginning of the line of music. That tells us that there are three flats in this key: B♭, E♭, and A♭. Don't worry about the A♭ and the B♭ in the pentascale, because five notes of the pentascale doesn't include the flats (that comes later, when we learn about eight-note scales in Chapter 9). But you do have to remember that every E in this key is an E♭. All of the examples in this chapter are written with the key signatures at the beginning of each line.

Let's look at another set of pentascales. The D Major pentascale contains D, E, F♯, G, and A.

The D minor pentascale contains the same notes, except for the third note. That F♯ has to be lowered half a step, so it becomes an F♮.

There are two ways to think about making minor pentascales. One is by starting with the notes of the major pentascale, and simply lowering the third by half a step. The second way to think about it is by understanding the pattern that makes up the minor pentascale. Just as with major pentascales, minor pentascales have a set pattern of steps and half steps. Once learned, these patterns make it easy to find all the patterns.

In the case of minor scales, we start with our root note, then go up a whole step (the *interval* of a second), then a half step, then a whole step, and then another whole step.

For example, staying in the key of D minor:

Start on D

Go up a whole step (E)

Go up a half step (F)

Go up a whole step (G)

Go up a whole step (A)

**UNIVERSAL LANGUAGE**

An **interval** in music refers to the distance between notes. In major chords, the distance between the first note of the chord and the second note of the chord is a major third: from the first note of the scale to the third note of the scale. In minor scales, it is a minor third. The distance of a third is two full steps. The distance of a minor third is a step and a half (because the third is lowered a half step to give it that minor sound).

Just as with the major scales, the root position chord is made up of the first note, the middle note, and the highest note of minor pentascale pattern (the root, the third, and the fifth). As with the major pentascales, a good way to practice these scales and chords is to play them going up the scale, then play them going down the scale, then play each note of the chord, and finally play the chord itself. Once you get comfortable, practice throwing down your hands on random notes and starting the pattern anywhere you happen to land.

All of the minor pentascales are written out for you to practice. As with the major pentascales, the key signatures at the beginning of each scale tell you which sharps and flats, if any, you need to use to play the pentascale. The minor five-finger positions that start on black notes can sometimes seem cramped. Be sure to keep your fingers in the middle of the keys, and be sure to maintain curved fingers.

*continues*

*continued*

**FLYING FINGERS**

Once you've started to get comfortable with the pentascales, try going back and forth between major and minor. Play the C Major pentascale followed by C minor, G Major followed by G minor, and so on.

Try doing this along with the metronome, to force you to think ahead and move quickly to each new position.

# Transposing Using Minor Pentascales

To transpose in a minor key, let's begin with the old folk song "The Erie Canal."

In A minor (the minor key with no sharps or flats):

 **Track 7, Example 3**

Now we are going to transfer the whole song to a different position: D minor. Notice that there are no flats or sharps in the first five notes of the D minor scale. (There is a B♭ in the D minor scale, but B♭ isn't one of the five pentascale notes, so we don't have to worry about it just yet.) Playing "The Erie Canal" in D minor is exactly the same as playing it in A minor, except that it starts on a different note.

But in other keys, there are sharps and flats. Let's consider C minor.

The C minor pentascale contains an E♭. So when we move "The Erie Canal" over to C minor, remember to play that E♭ in the middle.

# Minor Pentascale Exercises in All 12 Positions

As with the major pentascale exercises, the following exercises use different fingers in different sequences. First, learn the patterns as written by practicing two measures at a time. Then try to transpose them.

To remind you of the notes in each pentascale, the exercise begins with playing the notes of the five-finger position in order and ends with the chord. Remember to tell yourself the name of the chord as you play it.

**Track 8, Example 4**

Just like major pentascales, minor pentascales can be built on every note. As with the major pentascales, the advantage of practicing these exercises is that it is easy to apply the pattern in different keys. By staying in a five-finger pattern, you can concentrate on finger dexterity and not worry so much about music reading and finding the right notes.

# Two Hands at a Time

As in Chapter 4, first be sure that you haven't neglected your weaker hand when practicing the exercises in this chapter. Now put two hands together.

 **Track 9, Example 5**

# Improvisation Exercises

The improvisation exercise that follows gives you a chance to improvise in all the minor pentascales.

As with the major pentascale key improvisations, only the chords are written out—it's your job to improvise using the notes of the minor pentascales you have learned. The right-hand notation gives you the starting note. After the recorded example, you'll have four clicks on the metronome to get ready to play.

Track 10, Example 6

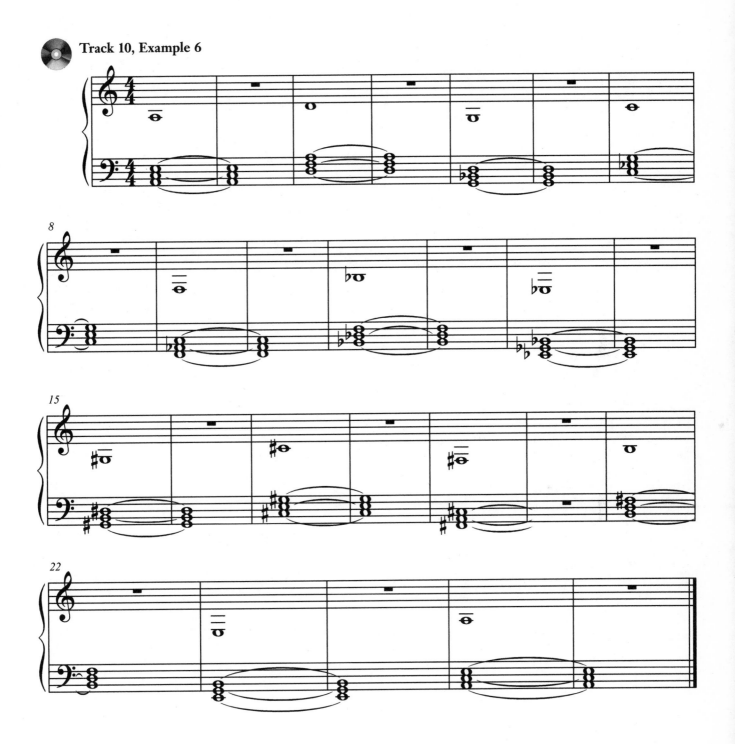

## The Least You Need to Know

- The minor pentascales are the same as the major pentascales, except that the third note of the pattern is lowered by half a step.
- The minor chord in any key is made up of the first, third, and fifth notes of the minor pentascale.
- Minor scales are often used in sad or somber music.

# Finger Gymnastics

## In This Chapter

- Moving beyond the five-finger position
- Learning to stretch and contract the hand to change position smoothly
- Practicing octave jumps and stretches
- Passing the thumb under the fingers and the fingers over the thumb

Earlier in the book, we talked about the pianist's hands and fingers as athletes. Now imagine your fingers are a team of gymnasts. Moving around in the pentascale positions and making basic three-note chords are equivalent to walking and running. Now we're going to teach our little gymnasts to move on to some beginning somersaults and maybe a cartwheel or two.

## Simple Moves

Getting comfortable at the keyboard not only involves teaching each finger which note to play and when to play it, it also involves being able to move the whole hand from one place on the piano to another. The simplest way to get comfortable with this is to practice playing the same pattern in different octaves. For example, you could start by playing the pentascale in C, then start the same pattern on a different C, then on yet a different C.

The key to jumping around the keyboard lies in thinking ahead. When you are playing one of the measure-long patterns in the following exercises, you should be looking ahead to the next measure, so that when it is time to move, you are ready to go.

All of the exercises are in a pentascale position, so they are good ones for you to transpose after you've learned them in the key of C. Note that the last two exercises in this section (the two-hand octave jumps) are extremely difficult to do with hands together if you haven't been playing the piano for a couple of years. So take them slowly, or learn them one hand at a time.

Let's start by practicing right-hand octave jumps. This simply means playing the same exercise in a different position—for example, eight notes higher or lower on the piano.

**THEORY AND PRACTICE**

A composer who wants the pianist to play the same pattern in two different octaves has two ways to write this instruction. Using standard notation, the composer simply writes the pattern out, and then writes it again using the notes of the new octave. Or the composer can use the symbol 8va (or 8vb) to tell the player to play the notes one octave higher than written (or, in the case of 8vb, one octave lower than written). The 8va and 8vb notations are often used on the very highest and very lowest notes of the piano, where the notes written in their standard placement can be difficult to read because of the many ledger lines.

**Track 11a, Example 1**

Now try the octave jumps in the left hand. These are important because the left hand does a lot of jumping around the keyboard in all kinds of music.

**Track 11b (0:27), Example 2**

The next challenge is to perform the octave jumps with both hands at the same time.

**Track 11c (0:59), Example 3**

**FLYING FINGERS**

It takes a while for pianists to get comfortable with big jumps on the piano. Octave jumps are common in all kinds of music, particularly in the left hand in waltz patterns and ragtime basses. Keep the following technique tips in mind as you practice:

- Read ahead! Forewarned is forearmed. If you read ahead, you will have more time to prepare and visualize the jump.

- Use the rests. If a composer gives you a half rest, don't wait until you are already supposed to be on the next note to start the move. Use the "free time" from the rest to put your hand in place.

- Move quickly off the starting note, and then hover over the landing note to give yourself time to be sure you come down accurately.

- Practice octave jumps from finger one to finger five. This is an interval that will soon feel very natural, as it is a comfortably stretched span for the average adult hand.

- You won't always be able to look at your moving hand, but use your peripheral vision to check your aim.

- Practice octave jumps with your eyes closed. It will teach you the feel of this important movement.

And finally, you're ready to try the most difficult octave jumps, where you play with both hands—and jump in opposite directions.

 **Track 11d (1:18), Example 4**

*continues*

*continued*

# Contracting the Hand

Up until now, we have followed the beginner's basic hand position rule of "one note for each finger." For example, when playing the C Major pentatonic scale, our thumb always played C, our second finger always played D, and so on.

There is a problem with this: the pianist has 10 fingers, and the piano has 88 keys. Clearly, our fingers need to be able to play more than one note if we are to use the entire range of the instrument.

One way to move the hand from position to position is to contract it. Let's take a simple five-finger pattern for the right hand, starting on C:

Notice that, just as in our five-finger positions in Chapter 4, the thumb plays C, the second finger plays D, the third finger plays E, the fourth finger plays F, and the fifth finger plays G.

Now however, we want to continue the pattern up the keyboard using completely different notes, so we are going to have to change hand positions entirely.

Performing this in a smooth and connected manner requires contracting the hand. When the fifth finger plays the G, hold it down and move your thumb so that it almost touches your pinky. The thumb will play the F right next door to G. Once the thumb has played F, allow the hand to relax so that it is once again in a five-finger position starting on the F. Repeat the pattern until your fifth finger gets to the next C. To continue moving up the keyboard, contract the hand so that the thumb can play B, and keep going.

To start, let's pause before we have to contract and start the next pattern.

 **Track 12a, Example 5**

Now let's try the same pattern backward. This time, you will pause when your thumb hits the last note of the pattern. Contract your hand so that you can bring the pinky down and place it next to the thumb to continue.

**Track 12b (0:13), Example 6**

In this next exercise, practice performing that contracting movement quickly. The change from one position to the next should be smooth, with no pause in between, as you go up and down the keyboard.

**Track 12c (0:27), Example 7**

The left hand can do the same exercise in reverse. As with the right hand, practice the one-measure patterns with pauses, until you can contract your hand in time.

 **Track 12d (0:54), Example 8**

In this exercise, playing hands together in contrary motion (opposite directions) is actually easier than playing in parallel motion (the same direction) because the fingers of each hand work as a mirror image of each other.

 **Track 12e (1:22), Example 9**

Finally, try playing in parallel motion. This may take some practice. Try to play cleanly—that is, with the fingers of both hands pressing the notes so that they sound in unison.

 **Track 12f (1:51), Example 10**

*continues*

*continued*

## Stretches

Stretching is another technique that lets the hand play more than five notes, and helps the pianist move from one place on the keyboard to another.

Stretching the thumb or pinky gives us the ability to play more notes without having to change position. In this first stretching exercise, the left-hand thumb stretches to be able to play more notes.

This pattern can also be turned into the familiar and ever-popular blues bass line.

**Track 13a, Example 11**

**Swing!** ♫ = ♩³♪

Now try a stretching exercise for the right hand. In the first line, the pinky stretches; in the second line, the thumb stretches.

Finally, try this common right-hand blues pattern, which requires starting in a five-finger position, then stretching the fingers of the right hand.

 **Track 13b (0:23), Example 12**

# Combining Contracting and Stretching

Combining contracting and stretching gives the pianist the ability to smoothly move over the entire keyboard.

The following exercise pattern is a hands-together exercise, but you should first start playing it with each hand separately. Don't try to rush this one—it's very difficult to play it quickly. A slow, deliberate tempo is fine. You're trying to train your hands to feel these intervals, not speed over them.

**Track 14, Example 13**

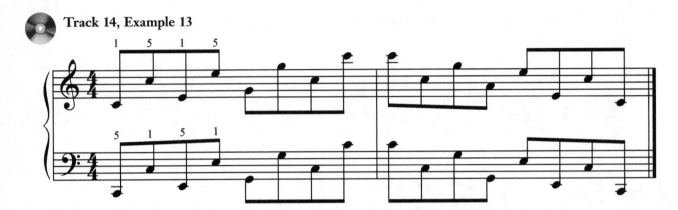

Here is another pattern that involves stretching and contracting. This pattern is found in music from virtually all periods, but it is especially common in the classical period. The fingering given offers a consistent pattern, but using the second finger instead of the third finger would also work; feel free to experiment here.

**Track 15, Example 14**

# Thumb Under, Fingers Over

Another technique that helps the pianist move around the keyboard is passing the thumb under the fingers, or moving the fingers over the thumb. Learning this movement is preparatory to playing scales, which we tackle in Part 3.

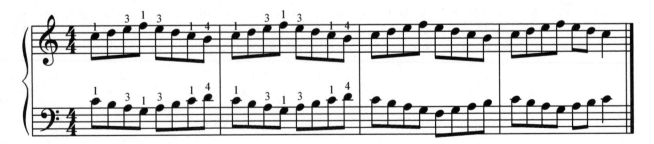

And here is a more challenging exercise to practice moving the thumb under the fingers, or the fingers over the thumb.

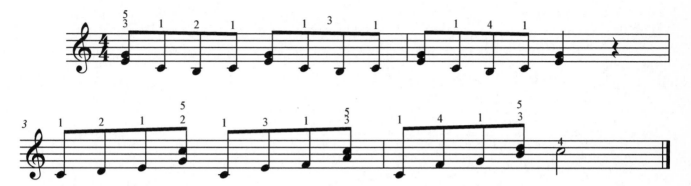

Finally, a left-hand exercise for thumb passes lets you move smoothly from one position to another while playing chords.

## The Least You Need to Know

- Keep your eyes on the music, not on your fingers, when practicing technique exercises.
- When jumping from one part of the keyboard to another, glance down briefly and plan your move before you need to perform it.
- Contracting and stretching the hand can be combined to allow the pianist to move smoothly over the entire keyboard.
- Passing the thumb under the fingers, or the fingers over the thumb, is another way to smoothly move from one position to another.

# More About Chords

## In This Chapter

- Practice exercises for chords in root position
- Common sequences of chords
- Chord inversions and arpeggios for learning fluency
- Common chord cadences in all major keys

One of the most important and obvious ways in which the piano differs from most other instruments (with the exception of the guitar and the organ) is its function as both a melodic and a harmonic instrument. You can play multiple notes at a time on the piano; you can play not only the tune of a song, but also its accompaniment. While some other instruments, such as the violin or cello, can play multiple notes at once, none rivals the piano as a solo instrument that can perform all the functions of music—a rhythm section, a harmony, and a melody—at the same time.

Chords are one of the foundations of piano playing. Essentially, a chord is any combination of three or more notes. Chords can be played in block form (all of the notes pressed down together at the same time) or in broken form (the notes are played one at a time), sometimes in a repeated pattern. Broken forms include repeated patterns, where the notes are played in a certain order; arpeggios, where the notes are played in sequence up and down the keyboard; and combinations of single notes and two or more notes played together.

Chapters 4 and 5 discussed how to make the basic major and minor chords in their root positions. The exercises in this chapter explore some of the many ways chords are used in different musical styles, as well as help you learn to move from one chord to another.

## Cross-Hand Arpeggios

Just as with single note playing, a number of techniques allow the pianist to smoothly move chords up and down the keyboard. Playing cross-hand arpeggios sounds much more difficult than it is, and has a dramatic impact on the piano's sound.

Start by playing a broken C chord with the left hand, followed by a broken C chord with the right hand.

**Track 16, Example 1**

Descending, the process is reversed. You may notice that, at first, going down the keyboard seems more difficult than going up the keyboard. This is because in your mind, you know you are playing a C chord, so you look for C as the starting note for each iteration of the pattern. Going downhill is like going backward, so you are looking for the top note of the chord (G), not the bottom note. Remind yourself of the chord notes as you practice this, and you will more quickly gain fluency. And of course, look before you leap.

Now go ahead and transpose the cross-hand arpeggio into all 12 major and minor keys.

Also, notice that the fingering feels a little cramped when starting on the black notes—yet another reason to play in the middle of the keys with rounded fingers.

 **SOUR NOTES**

Avoid using the sustain pedal (the one on the right) when practicing technique exercises. It's tempting to use the pedal with arpeggios, because the pedal gives arpeggios a big full sound, but it also covers up mistakes. You want to clearly hear what you are playing, so you can develop a nice, even touch.

# One-Octave Arpeggios

There are many times when you need to perform arpeggios with just one hand, as the other hand may be busy playing the melody. A one-octave arpeggio sounds full, and is used both by traditional composers and by pianists using a "fake book" to make up their own accompaniments. The basic root-position one-octave arpeggio consists of the basic chord plus the root note repeated at the top of the chord. To play all four notes, the hand has to spread out. To get the hang of playing in this position, play each of the all-white note arpeggios in the following exercise with your right hand and then your left hand, making sure to play with the fingerings as marked. You'll notice that some of these chords are major and some are minor. Right now, simply concern yourself with learning the fingering and becoming comfortable in this open-octave position.

The key issue in playing one-octave arpeggios is fingering. Fingering these patterns correctly may not seem crucial at the outset, but the standard fingerings have an important function in training the hand to play the notes in the most ergonomic position. Correct ergonomics is crucial not only for the one-octave patterns we are learning now, but also for the more complicated patterns we will learn in subsequent chapters.

Another issue is to let your wrist help you move your fingers so you are not in a fixed, stiff position. Your wrist should move loosely sideways so that the weight of each finger is above the note it is going to play.

## Right-Hand Arpeggio Fingerings

The right-hand fingerings for one-octave arpeggios are consistent for all major and minor chords. The arpeggios are played with the following fingers: 1–2–3–5–3–2–1.

Note that when you play multi-octave arpeggios later in this book, the right-hand arpeggios that start on black notes have a different fingering. But for a single octave, use the same fingering as you would for the white-note arpeggios.

Start by playing the major arpeggios. In this exercise, the chords are played chromatically, or one half step at a time.

Now try the minor arpeggios.

## Left-Hand Arpeggio Fingerings

Left-hand arpeggio fingerings aren't quite as consistent as right hand fingerings. The black-note arpeggios all use 5–3–2–1. With the white-note arpeggios, if the distance between the bottom note and the second note is a major third from a white note to a black note, then 5–3–2–1 is a better fit for most pianists' hands. If the interval is a major third from a white note to a white note, then 5–4–2–1 is the best fingering for most hands.

With minors, the fingerings are consistent: 5–4–2–1.

*continues*

*continued*

You can also practice these in different sequences:

- Alternating majors and minors
- Going through all the keys
- Two hands together

# Chord Inversions

Another way to vary chord practice is to play the same notes, but in a different order. The C chord, for example, comprises the notes C, E, and G. The C chord, however, can actually contain any C, any E, and any G on the entire piano. Choosing which particular notes to play is called "voicing." So the following chords are all C chords. As you play the following chords, listen carefully to how different the same chord can sound when played in different voicings.

Inverting a chord simply means playing the notes in sequence, but starting on a note other than the root. Instead of C–E–G, we can play E–G–C (first inversion) or G–C–E (second inversion).

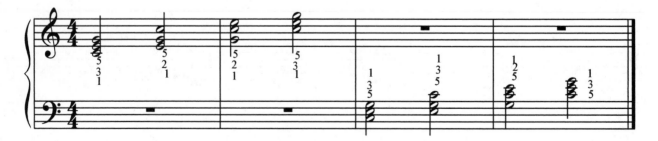

Practicing inversions will help you to become familiar with finding chords not only anywhere on the piano keyboard, but also in any position. The following exercises involve playing chords in different inversions. Remember: any given triad chord has only three notes in it, so remind yourself of those notes before you start. Other techniques that are applied here include contracting and expanding the hand. Be sure to use the correct finger on each note.

**Track 17, Example 2**

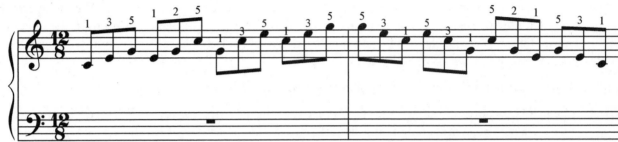

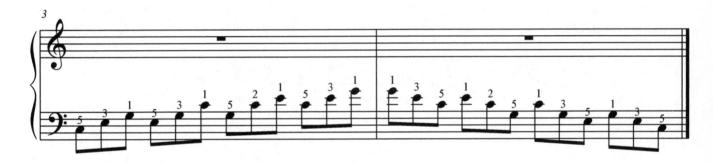

# Primary Chords in Different Keys

Looking at a new piece of music often seems as bewildering as reading in a different language. But in fact, just as in learning a new language, there are many repeated patterns within any given page of music. Once you learn what to look for, the patterns start to jump out at you.

For example, in most popular songs, about 80 percent of the harmonies (the chords) will probably be one of three primary chords, depending on the key the song is in. By learning which combination of chords commonly appear in the commonly used keys, pianists can quickly teach themselves to play literally thousands of popular songs.

## Finding the I, IV, and V Chords

Each key has a set of chords that are said to belong to that key. The most frequently used chords are called the primary chords. Most folk songs, blues songs, and many popular songs use only these chords. As a result, if you know that a song is in the key of C, and you know that the three primary chords in the key of C are C, F, and G, you know a great deal of the musical material needed to play that song.

Roman numerals are used to identify the chords in relation to the scale they are in. The chord that starts on the first note is the I, the chord that starts on the second note is a II, and so on. Notice some chords have capital letters; these are the major chords. Some have lowercase letters; these are the minors.

Also (as if things aren't confusing enough), some chords have numbers added, like V7. This means that, in addition to the three-note chord starting on the fifth note of the major scale, the chord contains an additional note. The numbers tell you which notes to add. So in the key of C, the V7 chord starts on G (the fifth note of the C scale). The 7 tells us to add the note that is seven notes up from the start of the chord. The start of the chord is G; seven notes up from G is F. Go ahead and count them up using only notes in our home key of C: G, A, B, C, D, E, F.

Believe it or not, this soon becomes automatic and you won't even have to think about it!

The primary chords are simply the chords that start on the first, fourth, and fifth notes of the scale. These chords can contain only notes that are in that scale. For example, in the key of G, the first note of the scale is G, the fourth note is C, and the fifth note is D. The I chord is G Major, which contains G, B, and D. The IV chord is C Major, which contains C, E, and G. The V chord is D major, which contains D, F♯, and A. Note that the V chord has to have the F♯ in it, because the key of G has an F♯ in it.

I    IV    V

In jazz, the primary chord sequence isn't the I–IV–V–I we've learned, but rather, ii–V–I.

The ii chord is a minor chord. In music theory, it is closely related to the IV chord. To make the ii chord, simply go to the second note of the major scale of the key in which you are playing and make a minor chord starting on that note. Keep in mind that this is a simplification. Jazz chords usually contain additional notes. If you decide to pursue jazz piano, you'll find that jazz theory books explain how to add more notes to chords to get a more complex sound.

Here are the primary chords in all 12 major keys, written with sharps and flats rather than key signatures. For each sequence of chords, practice using the following patterns. The patterns are written in C Major for clarity, but you should practice the cadences in each key by transposing the patterns into each key.

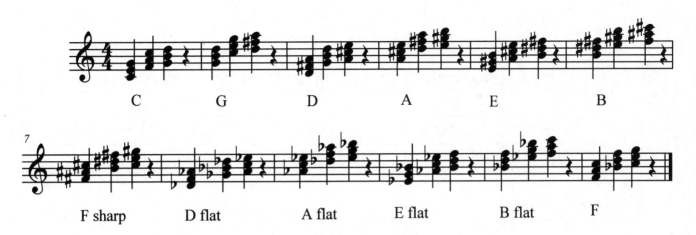

C    G    D    A    E    B

F sharp    D flat    A flat    E flat    B flat    F

Skilled pianists can play chords up and down the keyboard. The following patterns, written out in C, can be applied to each group of primary chords. In the exercises written with hands together, start by learning them with hands apart.

 **Track 18, Example 3**

*continues*

## Cadences

The primary chords often form the backbone of musical compositions, especially folk and popular songs. But even master classical composers such as Chopin have entire pages filled with nothing in the left hand but primary chords. The cadence is a series of these primary chords: I–IV–I–V7–I.

Composers and improvisers usually use primary chords in voicings that are pleasant to listen to. This means that instead of bouncing all over the piano, the pianist or composer uses the inversions that are right next to each other. In the following example, note that the first cadence jumps around, while the second cadence stays in one place. They both use the same notes, but the second version sounds more like a choir.

**Track 19, Example 4**

Notice that the voiced cadence in the previous exercise includes a four-note chord, which is called the V7. In the following exercises, that note is added right after the V chord is played.

*continues*

*continued*

## The Least You Need to Know

- Chords are made up of three or more notes.
- The notes of a chord can be played in any order, all over the piano.
- Chords are commonly found in groups of primary chords, according to the key the music is in.
- The I, IV, and V7 chord form a common cadence, or series of chords.

# Scaling the Heights

Part

3

Scales are the basis for Western music, whether it's Bach or Bachman Turner Overdrive. And it's not just about "Do Re Mi." Sure, we start with major scales. But we're going to hit minor scales (all three kinds), modes, and chromatic, whole-tone, blues, and pentatonic scales. You'll learn how to make the scales and how to finger them.

Most of all, you're going to learn how to *use* them. Scales are simply collections of notes that sound good together, and they provide most of the notes used in a piece in any given key. When you know your scales, you can improvise for hours, or use them as the basis for making your own music. How? Read on ....

# Major Scales

## In This Chapter

- Making the major scale
- Fingering groups for major scales
- Practice tips for scales
- Using scales in music

The major scale is the foundation of the *diatonic system,* which is the basic organization of notes used in Western music. The major scale was discussed in Chapter 4 when you learned the five-note penta-scale patterns. The full eight-note major scale includes those five notes, plus three more. It's the full "Do-Re-Mi" scale from the *Sound of Music.* Or hum the first eight notes of "Joy to the World" (The Christmas song, not "Jeremiah Was a Bullfrog")—it's the major scale played backward.

Major scales have seven different notes, with "Do" repeated as the scale's bottom note and top note. So we think of scales as having eight notes. To play eight notes with five fingers is clearly impossible, unless we change positions so that we can reach the additional notes. Thus, mastering scales requires mastering the technique of passing the thumb under the fingers or the fingers over the thumb, as you learned in Chapter 6, to smoothly shift positions.

## Construction of Scales

Like pentascales, major scales can be built on any note on the piano. To start, we've chosen the C scale because with no black notes, it's the easiest scale to visualize on the piano. A major scale on any other note will have its own unique combination of white and black notes to create that familiar Do-Re-Mi sound.

There are many ways to learn scales. Some people learn them by memorizing patterns or notes. Others poke at the piano and find the notes by ear, which, while it may be an effective way to find a scale, is not an efficient way to actually learn it. Some people learn the pattern of half steps and whole steps (as you did with the pentascales).

The **diatonic system** refers to music that is composed using notes from the major scale or related scales such as the minors described in Chapter 9. Other notes may be used to help move the piece from key to key, or as decoration. The vast majority of classical music until the twentieth century, and most popular music, is composed using the diatonic system.

Every major scale is constructed as follows:

- Starting tone is Do
- Go up a whole step to Re
- Go up a whole step to Mi
- Go up a half step to Fa
- Go up a whole step to Sol
- Go up a whole step to La
- Go up a whole step to Ti
- Go up a half step to Do

Let's look at a few scales.

In the key of C:

- Starting tone is Do (C)
- Go up a whole step to Re (D)
- Go up a whole step to Mi (E)
- Go up a half step to Fa (F)
- Go up a whole step to Sol (G)
- Go up a whole step to La (A)
- Go up a whole step to Ti (B)
- Go up a half step to Do (C)

In the key of A♭:

- Starting tone is Do (A♭)
- Go up a whole step to Re (B♭)
- Go up a whole step to Mi (C)
- Go up a half step to Fa (D♭)
- Go up a whole step to Sol (E♭)
- Go up a whole step to La (F)
- Go up a whole step to Ti (G)
- Go up a half step to Do (A♭)

Now try to find the notes of the scales starting on other notes. Don't worry about playing them smoothly or fingering them just yet—that comes next. Right now, just get comfortable with the idea that scales have different combinations of white notes and black notes, and that you can find them using a pattern that works for every key.

# Scale Fingering Groups

Many pianists are surprised to learn that there are far more possible fingerings for playing scales than the standard fingerings we are most commonly taught (and which, it should be noted, you'll find in this book).

In actual music, scale passages rarely start on the first note of the scale and end on the eighth note. Instead, they may start on any note of the scale; they may run a few notes up, and then a lot of notes down; they may run a lot of notes up, and then a few notes down; they may stop and start anywhere; and they may change direction. They may even involve the introduction of a few notes that aren't in the scale. Each variation can necessitate changes in fingering.

In fact, the common scale fingerings used today—with the thumb passing under the fingers to bring the hand to a new position—weren't used very often in the Baroque period (the early-to-middle eighteenth century). Instead, Baroque keyboard players often passed the second or third finger over the other fingers—a fingering technique that is rarely used today in scale passages (although this fingering is often used in Baroque pieces to achieve a smooth and connected so-called "legato" touch).

So why bother learning the so-called "correct" fingerings for scales if they don't usually appear in music that way and they can be altered in so many other ways?

Quite simply, we need a starting point. The brain learns to play quick passages by repeating the exact same movements over and over. By using the same fingerings, we develop fluency. We can later vary what we are doing with other fingerings. But first, we need to achieve a base level of technical facility.

 **FLYING FINGERS**

There are a few rules that are common for playing all scales. Try to keep these in mind:

- Never skip a finger.
- Avoid putting the thumb on a black note.
- As you go up or down a scale, the thumbs alternate whether they cross under the third or fourth finger.
- As you go up or down a scale, the third and fourth fingers take turns crossing over the thumbs.

In addition to fingering rules that apply to all scales, the 12 major scales can be organized in groups that use similar fingerings. By practicing the scales in fingering groups, we solidify each set of fingering patterns before moving on to the next.

## White Note Fingerings

The first group is the white key group: scales starting on white keys. This set of fingerings works for all of the major white note scales with the exception of B and F. (It also works for five of the seven minor scales that start on white notes, which we will discuss in Chapter 9.) The scales in this group are C, G, D, A, and E.

The fingering elements of this set of scales are as follows:

- The right hand starts the scale on the thumb and ends on the fifth finger.

- The left hand starts on the fifth finger and ends on the thumb.

- When playing hands together, the third fingers always play at the same time.

 **Track 20, Example 1**

*C Major*

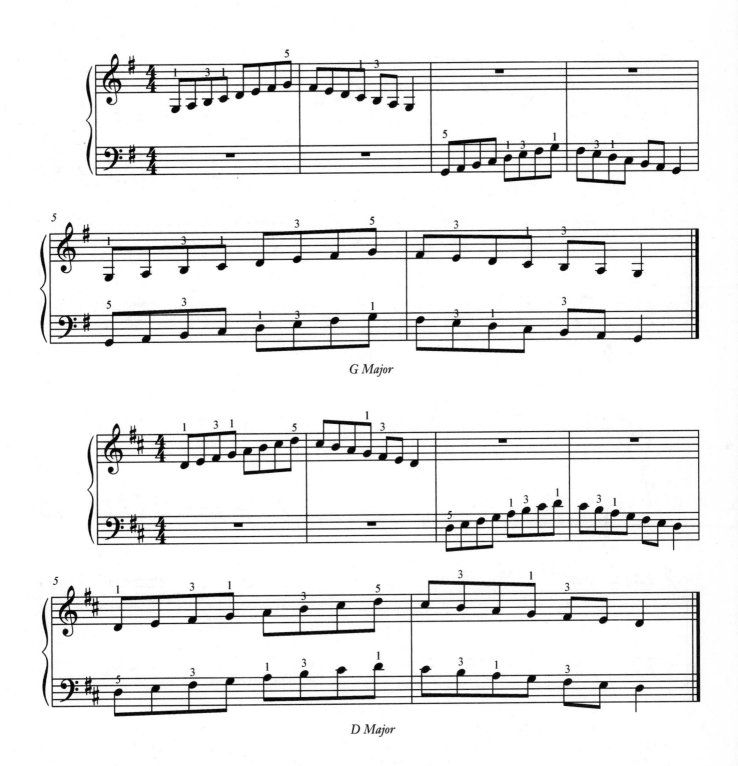

*G Major*

*D Major*

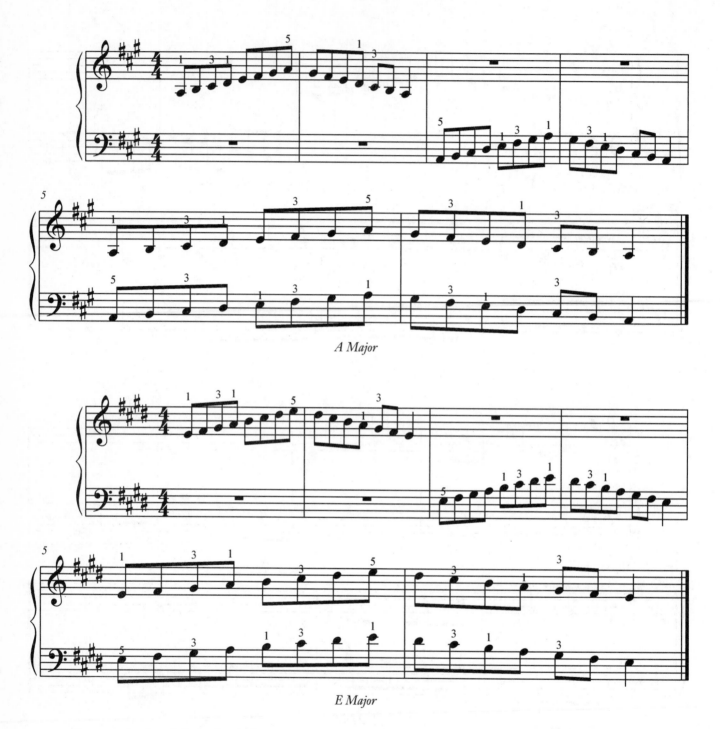

*A Major*

*E Major*

Once you've learned to play eight-note scales up and down, it's time to play two-octave scales. The trickiest part of playing two-octave scales with hands together is negotiating the beginning of the second octave.

Here are some tips for fingering the transition to the second octave:

- When you get to the second octave, both thumbs will play the tonic (root) note at the same time.

- The fourth finger of either hand only plays next door to the tonic; the third finger does not play next to the tonic.

- Do not skip fingers, and the third fingers always play together.

- Practice the "turnaround" section by itself. Notice that both the left hand and the right hand use the following fingering:

  - Ascending: The left hand plays 2–1–4; the right hand plays 4–1–2
  - Descending: The left hand plays 4–1–2; the right hand plays 2–1–4

Now try the two-octave scales in the keys of C, G, D, A, and E.

 **Track 21, Example 2**

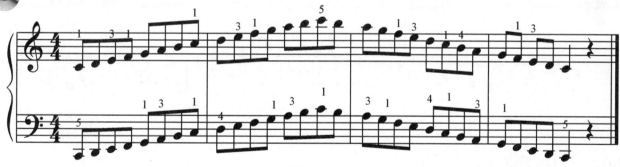

*C Major scale*

*G Major scale*

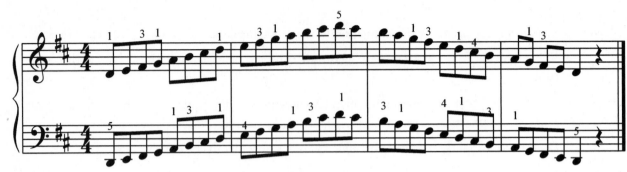

*D Major scale*

*A Major scale*

*E Major scale*

## Black Note Scales

The second fingering group is composed of black note scales, with the exception of F♯ (or G♭). These scales are actually easier to play fluently, because the thumb easily passes under fingers that are on black notes.

Follow these fingering rules:

- In the right hand, the fourth finger always and only plays the B♭. (Note: the sole exception is the starting note of the B♭ scale, which, for ergonomic reasons, can also be played with the fourth finger—or with the second or third finger. It's your choice, although I've fingered it with a "four" to keep things consistent.)

- In the left hand, the third finger starts the scale and the fourth finger always plays the fourth note of the scale.

- As with white note scales, the transitions over and under the third and fourth fingers alternate.

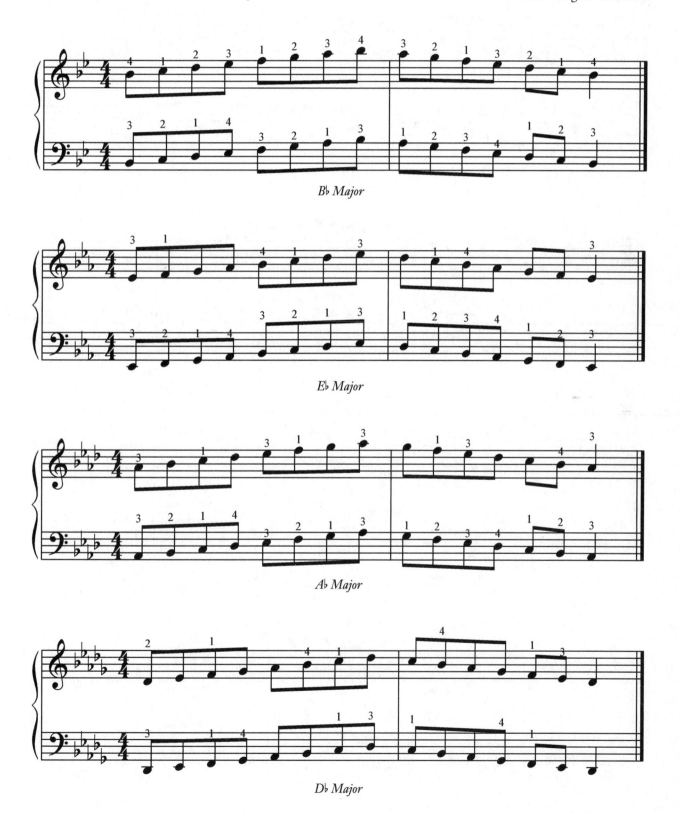

*B♭ Major*

*E♭ Major*

*A♭ Major*

*D♭ Major*

As with white note scales, practice the black note scales one octave hands apart, one octave hands together, two octaves hands apart, and two octaves hands together.

*B♭ Major scale*

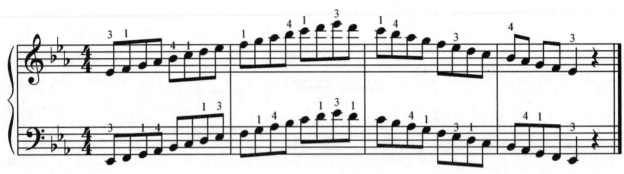

*E♭ Major scale*

*A♭ Major scale*

*D♭ Major scale*

## Leftover Scales Group: B, F, F♯

The final group contains scales that break the preceding rules because of where their sharps and flats fall.

The right hand of the F scale follows the black-note scale rule of playing the fourth finger on the B♭—while the left hand follows the white-note scale rule of starting with the pinky.

The B scale has the opposite issue: the right hand follows the normal right-hand fingering rules, while the left hand is forced to start on the fourth finger because of the F♯.

Finally, the F♯ scale follows the right-hand rule for black note scales. Keep in mind that A♯ is enharmonic (the same note) as B♭. So as with the black note scales, the fourth finger of the right hand plays the A♯. But the left hand is different because of the placement of the black notes: it starts on the fourth finger. In the key of F♯, the left-hand fingers all play on black notes, while the thumb plays on the white notes.

## Practicing Scales

Scales make excellent warm-up exercises. They should be played smoothly, in time, and with no fingering mishaps. A good way to incorporate scales into your daily practice is to play the scale of a piece or song you are practicing before starting to practice that piece of music.

> **SOUR NOTES**
>
> When practicing scales, don't try to fix fingering mistakes on the fly. Your job is to internalize the correct fingerings. Fixing mistakes on the fly usually means correcting one incorrect fingering with a compensating incorrect fingering, meaning that you are practicing mistakes. When you make a mistake, go back to the beginning of either the ascending or descending scale where you made the mistake and try again.

Here are a few tips for practicing scales:

- Tackle one scale at a time. They get easier with practice.

- Start with one hand at a time, one octave ascending and descending. Practice until you can play the scale with your eyes closed.

- Play one-octave scales, hands together.

- As soon as possible, practice two octaves up and down so that you get practice with all the fingering changes.

- Do this with hands apart until you can play each hand with your eyes closed.

- Practice the scales in fingering groups.

Scales are used in music in a variety of different ways. They can start and end on any note, they can change directions, and they can include other notes, requiring refingering. They also can be played against a variety of left-hand accompaniments.

 **Track 22, Example 3**

The following exercise contains two different left-hand patterns against a right-hand scale.

Once you've mastered the previous example and can play the scales solidly in all the keys, try the exercise in different keys, playing the scales in the right hand and the accompanying pattern in the left hand. You can also flip the hands so that the left hand plays scales while the right hand plays an accompaniment. But don't rush this; it takes time.

## The Least You Need to Know

- All major scales use the same combination of steps and half steps to create the Do-Re-Mi scale sound.
- Learn scales in groups that use the same fingerings.
- In all scales, the thumb passages alternate between the third and fourth fingers.
- Scale passages used in music often start, end, and change direction on different notes.

# Minor Scales

## In This Chapter

- The relationship between major and minor scales
- Making the natural minor scale
- Making the harmonic minor scale
- Making the melodic minor scale

Chapter 5 explored the basic nature of the minor pentascale, the five-note pattern that—with its lowered third note—sounds a bit sadder, darker, and more somber than a major pentascale.

Like major scales, minor scales have seven different notes (eight notes, if we consider that we start on Do and end on Do).

# Playing the Natural Minor Scale

Just as a major scale can start on any of the 12 notes, a minor scale can start on each of the 12 notes. As it turns out, each major scale has a "relative" minor scale, meaning that there is a minor scale that shares the same key signature (the same number of flats and sharps). In every case, the relative minor scale starts on the sixth note of the major scale.

For instance, in the key of C, the notes of the scale are C, D, E, F, G, A, B, and C. The sixth note of this scale is A. Therefore, A minor is the relative minor of C.

What this means is that the key of A minor shares all of the same notes as the key of C Major. (C Major has only white notes, so A minor has only white notes.) The only difference is that instead of starting and ending on C, the A minor scale starts and ends on A.

 **Track 23, Example 1**

C Major Scale          A minor Scale

Let's take the key of E Major. C♯ is the sixth note of the E Major scale, so C♯ is the relative minor of E Major.

E Major Scale          C♯ minor Scale

# Fingering Groups for the Minor Scales

As with the major scales, the minor scales can be divided into fingering groups. The same fingering rules that applied to major white note scales apply to the white note fingering groups; the black notes are a bit muddled because of the placement of the sharps and flats. But after doing all the scale work in Chapter 8, chances are that the minor scales will come very quickly because your fingers are already used to working in these patterns.

The white-note fingering group of minor scales include the following:

A minor

C minor

D minor

E minor

G minor

The black-note fingering group of minor scales include the following:

D♭ minor

E♭ minor

G♭ minor

G♯ minor

B♭ minor

That leaves two scales left over, so we'll put them in their own little group:

F minor

B minor

Just like the major note scales, practice these scales in the following sequence:

1. One hand at a time, one-octave scales

2. Hands together, one-octave scales

3. Hands apart, two-octave scales

4. Hands together, two-octave scales

Once you can play two-octave scales, playing three- and four-octave scales is simply a matter of repeating what you've already done.

The minor scales are notated a little later in this chapter. First, though, there are some variations you need to know.

# Variations on the Minor Scale

The scales described in the previous section are called the natural minor scales. As it turns out, there are two important variations on minor scales, both of which are commonly used by composers. Both contain slight variations involving the sixth and seventh notes of the scales. The fingerings for the harmonic and most melodic minor scales are the same as those for the natural minor scales.

**FLYING FINGERS**

Practice minor scales in a sequence of natural minor, melodic minor, and harmonic minor. The basic fingerings are the same, with only rare exceptions for some of the melodic minor scales. Practicing the scales in groups solidifies the fingerings while teaching you to make slight variations using the different chromatic notes required by the different scales. Because this is the way composers use scales—with variations—this is good training.

## Playing the Harmonic Minor Scale

In the harmonic minor scale, the seventh note of the scale is raised by half a step, giving the scale a Middle Eastern feel. You can imagine gypsy dancers or a snake charmer accompanied by music played in this scale. The harmonic minor scale is used in music throughout the world, and it is extremely common in classical Western music.

Look at the A minor scale and compare the natural minor to the harmonic minor. Note that the harmonic minor has a G♯ instead of a G, which leads more strongly to the final A note.

 **Track 24a, Example 2**

A natural minor     A harmonic minor

**THEORY AND PRACTICE**

The harmonic minor scale is so named because it enables the composer to work with harmonies that reinforce the sense of the key in which they are writing. In the key of A minor, the raised G♯ is called the "leading tone" because it leads so strongly to the A. When harmonizing this note, the composer would choose to use a chord that contains a G♯, rather than a chord that contains a G natural. The E chord, for example, would be used rather than E minor, and this chord has the harmonic function of leading back to the home key of A. Because of this harmonic function, this scale is called the harmonic minor.

## Playing the Melodic Minor Scale

The third type of minor scale is the melodic minor scale. Just as the harmonic minor scale is altered for harmonic reasons, the melodic minor scale can be said to have a melodic function. In the melodic minor scale, the sixth and seventh notes are raised going up, and they return to the natural form going down.

In fact, composers use notes from the melodic minor scale every which way—going uphill and downhill and often using them chromatically. Composers, after all, do not write with music theory textbooks in hand. The melodic minor scale is especially common in jazz.

**Track 24b (0:09), Example 3**

A natural minor                           A melodic minor

**THEORY AND PRACTICE**

The melodic minor scale makes sense for voice leading reasons. Going uphill, the raised sixth and seventh seem to lead more insistently to the target note of the tonic. Going downhill, lowering them to the natural sixth and seventh seems to lead more easily to the fifth. These intervals are easier for singers to manage. For pianists, some of the scales require using different fingerings going up and down because the notes are different.

The following music examples show all the minor scales: single octaves for natural, melodic, and harmonic minor scales, and a two-octave scale for the natural minor scale. It is an easy adaptation to then practice the melodic and harmonic minor scales in two octave runs—or three or four octave runs, if you choose. Except for the first scale, in which all finger changes are given, fingerings are given for the natural minor scale, but not repeated for the harmonic and melodic scales unless there are differences. Fingerings are also provided for two-octave scales.

A minor

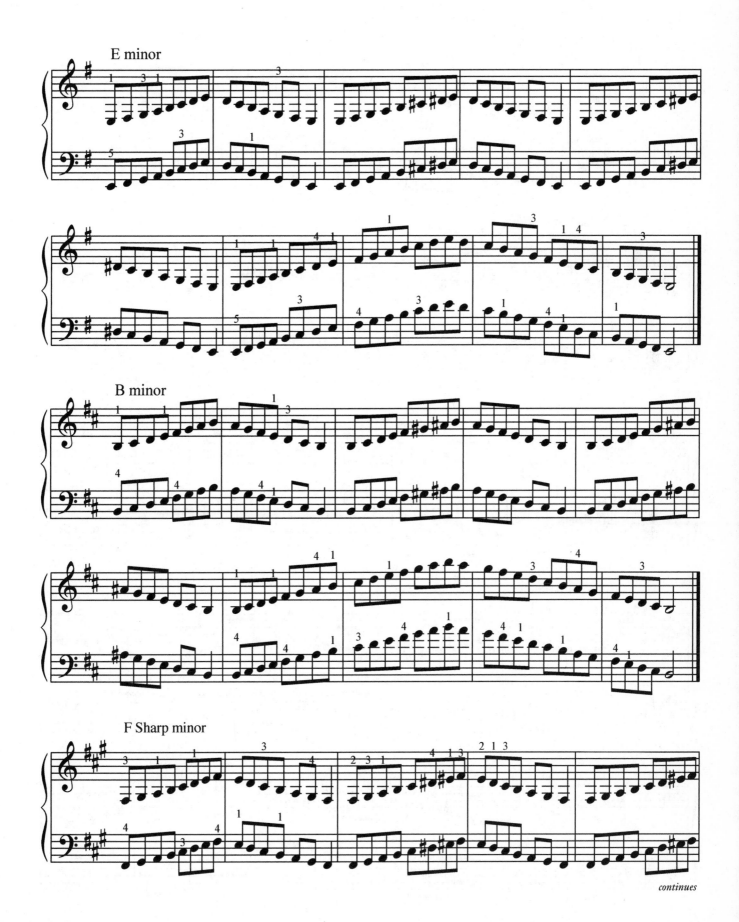

*continues*

*continued*

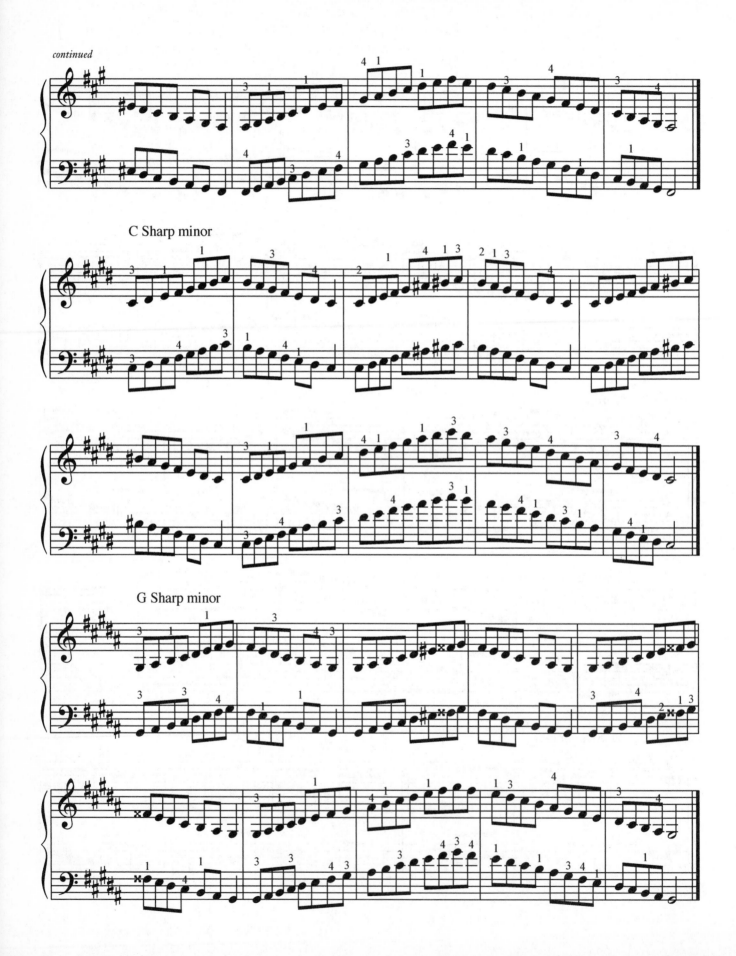

C Sharp minor

G Sharp minor

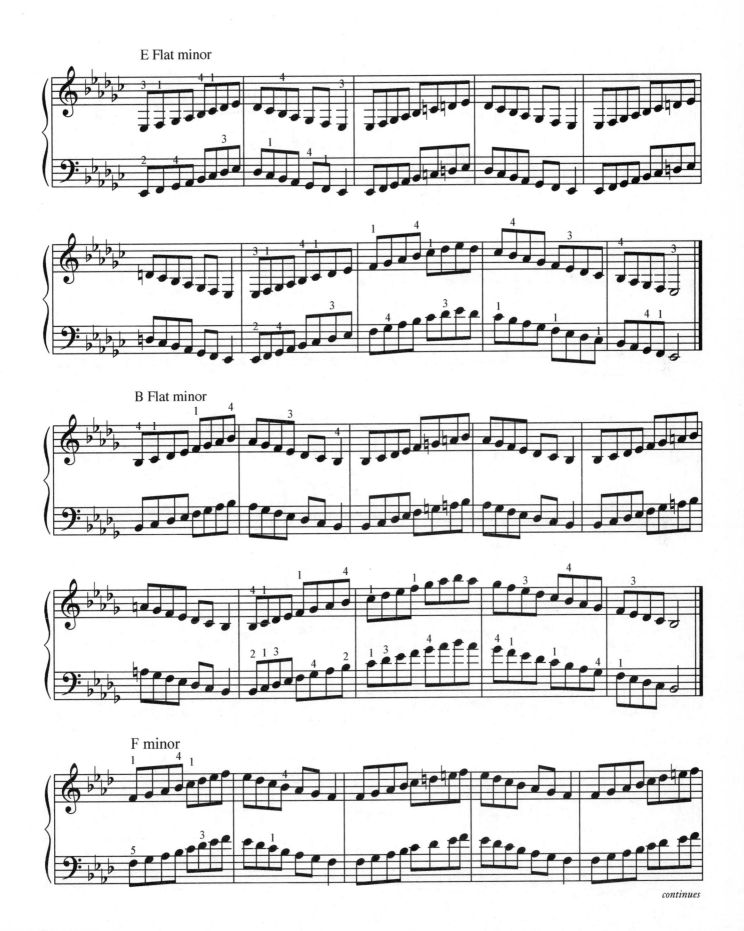

E Flat minor

B Flat minor

F minor

*continues*

*continued*

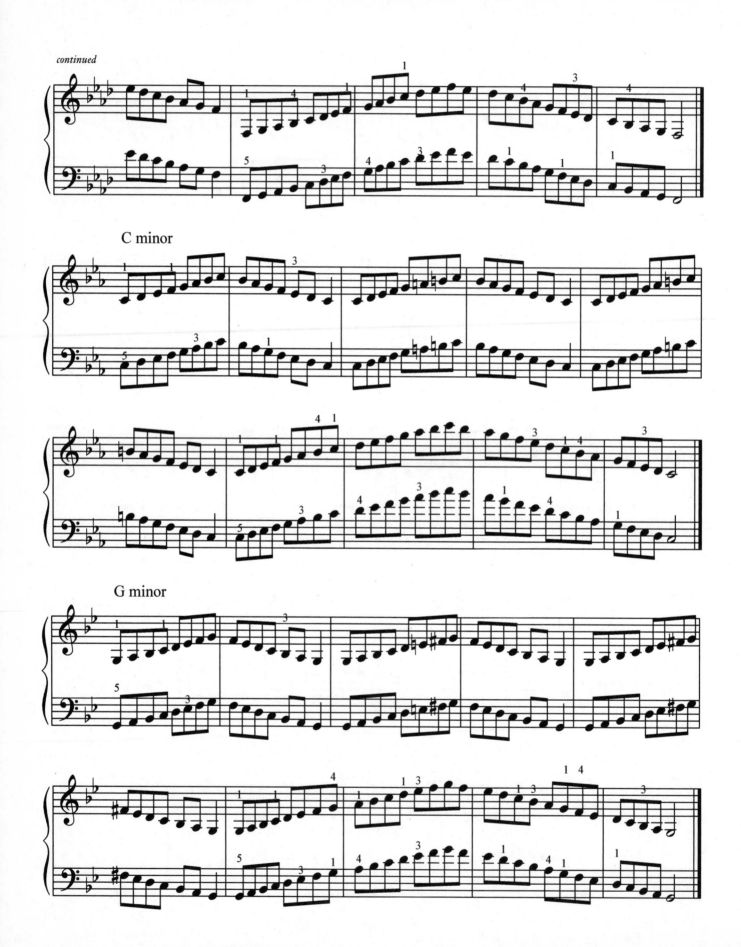

C minor

G minor

D minor

## The Least You Need to Know

- Every major scale has a related natural minor scale, which uses the exact same notes but starts on the sixth note of the major scale.

- In the harmonic minor scale, the seventh note is raised half a step, giving it a Middle Eastern sound.

- In the melodic minor scale, the sixth and seventh notes are raised when ascending the scale; the natural minor scale is used when descending.

# Music à la Mode

## In This Chapter

- Learning the names, notes, and sounds of the seven modes
- Learning modes in all keys
- Playing modes with chords
- Improvising exercises for modes

So far, we've learned that each of the 12 notes has its own major scale, and three forms of the minor scale. But wait! There's more ….

Modes are variations on scales. They are frequently used in jazz as the basis for improvisation, and they also are common in runs and scale passages in classical music. There is perhaps no better way of developing keyboard fluency than learning to play in all modes of all the keys.

At first, it looks intimidating: modes seem to either fascinate or repel music students. Some students are intrigued by the seeming complexity; others take one look and declare the whole matter incomprehensible.

Both reactions are extreme because modes are much simpler than they appear. Essentially, a mode means starting a scale on a different note. In other words, starting a C scale on any note other than C and using the notes of the C scale. Go ahead and try it. Play all the white notes, but instead of playing from C to C, play from D to D. There, you've done it. You've played a mode.

It wasn't so hard, was it?

## The Mode Names

Perhaps the most complicated thing about modes is their names. So let's get it over with. Here are the names of the modes and their descriptions:

- The Ionian mode starts on the first note of the major scale, making it just another name for the regular old major scale.
- The Dorian mode starts and ends on the second note of the major scale.
- The Phrygian mode starts and ends on the third note of the major scale.
- The Lydian mode starts and ends on the fourth note of the scale.
- The Mixolydian scale starts and ends on the fifth note of the scale.
- The Aeolian mode starts and ends on the sixth note of the scale.
- The Locrian mode starts and ends on the seventh note of the scale.

To cut straight through all of these names to the actual music, simply play a C scale. Then play the same notes, but instead of playing from C to C, play from D to D. That's your D Dorian scale. Now play from E to E; that's Phrygian. F to F is Lydian. G to G is the Mixolydian. A to A is Aeolian (and notice, too, that because A is the sixth note of the C Major scale, this mode is identical to the natural minor scale). The final mode, Locrian, goes from B to B, and is rarely used.

**FLYING FINGERS**

Mode names were established in the Middle Ages, and refer to the modes thought to be used in Ancient Greece. The truth, however, is that no one—including the monks of the Middle Ages—actually knows or knew what notes the Ancient Greeks used in their modes, or what their modes sounded like. As a result of a medieval fascination with the idea of Ancient Greece, we have inherited complicated-sounding words like Mixolydian to describe what is really a simple idea: starting a scale on a different note.

Listen to how changing the first and last ending notes of the scale completely changes the sound and nature of the sequence, even though all the notes are the same. This change of character is what is interesting about the modes, and what makes them such a powerful tool for improvisation.

Now go ahead and play the modes of the C scale while playing the matching chord. What matching chord? Well, the Dorian mode starts on D, so you need a chord that starts on D. You can use the notes only in the parent scale, which is C major. So the chord that starts on D has to be a D minor chord, containing D, F, and A, all of which are from the C Major (parent) scale.

The Phrygian mode starts on E, so play the E minor chord. (Same deal: you need E, G, and B, all of which are found in the C Major scale). For Lydian, play the F Major chord. And so on.

**Track 25, Example 1**

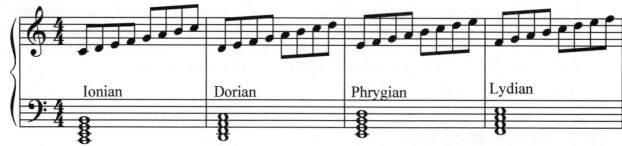

At first, modes may seem a little more complicated when you start moving into keys with more sharps and flats. Try finding all the modes in the key of E♭.

We start with the E♭ major scale.

So looking at the E♭ major scale, we can see the following:

- The Ionian mode (or parent scale) starts on E♭
- The Dorian mode starts on F
- The Phrygian mode starts on G
- The Lydian mode starts on A♭
- The Mixolydian mode starts on B♭
- The Aeolian mode starts on C
- The Locrian mode starts on D

Now it's your turn to find all the modes and their associated chords in each scale. This is an exercise that takes time to master and internalize. Progress of one mode per week is good and solid.

**THEORY AND PRACTICE**

Modes are considered major or minor based on whether the distance from the first note to the third note is a major third or a minor third.

The Ionian, Lydian, and Mixolydian scales are major.

The Dorian, Phrygian, Aeolian, and Locrian scales are minor.

# Practicing and Improvising with Modes

Modes are easy to practice and satisfying as well, because each mode has a distinctive sound and feel. Using them in improvisation exercises offers limitless ways to explore the sounds of the different modes and connect them in different musical combinations. This is also a great way to apply scales to actual music, because scales are more likely to show up in varied forms such as modes than as straight major or minor scales running up and down the keyboard.

This is one place where the pianist should feel free to experiment with different fingerings. Of course, you can use the standard fingering from the parent major scale. But you can also choose fingerings from other scales, usually depending on what the music is actually doing. Often, using a fingering that belongs to the major scale that starts on the same note will work. Sometimes, the placement of sharps or flats will make a fingering impossible, and you'll need to vary it, applying the same general fingering patterns you learned with the major and minor scales. The point of these exercises is not to practice a rigid set of fingerings with a whole other assortment of scales, but rather to apply fingering techniques you've used to the different modes so that you can play comfortably in all keys.

In each of the following exercises, use your left hand to play a chord and the right hand to play a mode associated with that chord. Then continue playing the series of chords with the left hand, while using the right hand to improvise using the mode associated with the chord.

For visual clarity, let's start in the key of C. After you are comfortable in the key of C, you can start transposing the mode exercises into other keys. At first, it will be easier to remember the modes and their notes in keys with fewer black notes.

**FLYING FINGERS**

Here are some tips for practicing the modes:

- Practice one group of modes at a time. It's too confusing to tackle more than one new scale and all of its modes.
- Start in the simpler keys: C (of course), then G, then D, and finally F.
- Choose keys that match the keys of songs or pieces you are practicing.
- For jazz players, E♭, B♭, and A♭ are important and common keys.
- Play in time. As always, using the metronome forces you to think more quickly to find the right notes.
- At the beginning, start and end your improvisations on the starting note of the mode so that you have a clear feel for the tonal center.

Many of the examples in this chapter are written with left-hand chords and right-hand scales because that is the way modes are most commonly used in improvising. Classical pianists, however, would do well to reverse the exercises and also practice modes with the left hand, because mode runs are often found in the left hand as well as the right, and because practicing modes teaches dexterity and keyboard geography.

The following mode exercise is designed to familiarize the player with all the modes in all keys, along with their related chords.

Notice that while the right hand is playing the modes in the following examples, the left hand is playing a related chord.

Also notice the use of seventh chords in this example. This will help you become more familiar with these more complex and interesting-sounding chords. If using seventh chords seems overwhelming at first, feel free to just play the basic triad, the bottom three notes of any of the chords in the following example.

You will hear immediately that this sequence of chords is very musical, and seems to progress logically from one chord to the next, making it easier to improvise something that is musically satisfying. And indeed, this type of chord progression can be found buried in music throughout the last 200 (or more) years.

In the following exercise, the modes are simply played over their related chords three times. The first time through, the mode is simply played as a scale. The second time, it is played as noted on the sheet music. The third time is an improvisation (not noted on the sheet music). Then it's your turn to improvise. You'll be given four metronome clicks to cue you in, and then you'll have eight beats to improvise over each chord in the progression. The recorded example shows how this is done in the key of C.

The first exercise is written in the key of C, and includes all seven modes in the following sequence:

- The first measure starts on the I chord and uses the Ionian mode.

- The second measure starts on the IV chord and uses the Lydian mode.

- The third measure starts on the vii chord and uses the Locrian mode.

- The fourth measure starts on the iii chord and uses the Phrygian mode.

- The fifth measure starts on the vi chord and uses the Aeolian mode.

- The sixth measure starts on the ii chord and uses the Dorian mode.

- The seventh measure starts on the V chord and uses the Mixolydian mode.

- The last measure returns to the home key.

**Track 26, Example 2**

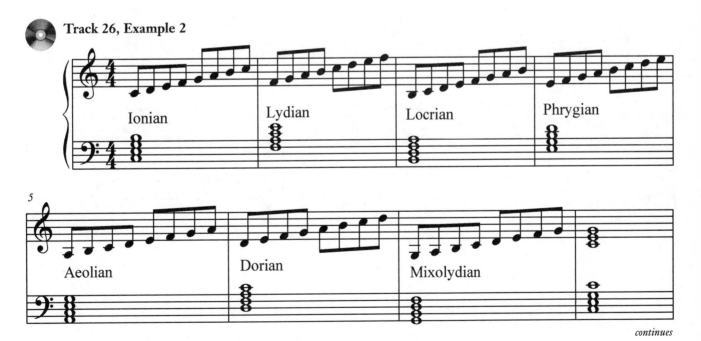

*continues*

*continued*

Continue playing the same chord progression in the left hand while improvising in the right hand using the notes of the mode. Each chord should get eight beats (two measures).

Once you're comfortable in the key of C, it's time to transpose this exercise, play through the chord cycle, and improvise over it in all of the keys. This example shows how it would be transposed to the key of E♭ Major.

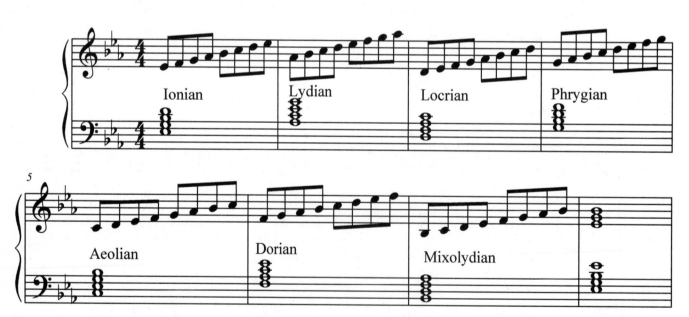

Continue playing the same chord progression in the left hand while improvising in the right hand using the notes of the mode. Each chord should get eight beats (two measures).

The mode exercises in this chapter may take weeks to master, depending on your level and how much time you put in. Don't despair. Nothing says you have to learn them all at once. You'll probably find that after you've learned three or four keys, the next few seem much easier. This is because your brain will start to recognize the patterns.

## The Least You Need to Know

- Playing a "mode" means playing the notes of a scale starting on a different note.
- Modes have a very different sound than the parent scales, and are used in both improvisation and classical composition.
- Fingerings for playing modes follow the basic fingering rules that apply to other seven-note scales, but can often be adjusted to account for the presence of sharps and flats in different places.
- Practice the modes in groups, one key at a time.

# Singing the Blues

Perhaps no scale has influenced the music of the twentieth century and beyond as much as a scale that was never even written down in music notation until long after it found its way to America on slave ships from Africa.

A simple series of six notes, the blues scale revolutionized first American—and then worldwide—popular music. It has found its way into country, rock, jazz, and folk, and in every permutation and combination imaginable.

Originally, blues was not performed on a keyboard instrument, or for that matter, on any sort of instrument. At its earliest, it was a vocal song form, and it remains so to this day. One of the things that gives the blues its characteristic sound are notes that are sometimes said to exist between the cracks of the piano keys. In other words, these notes don't have an exact equivalent in the Western diatonic scale. On a piano keyboard, you can't bend the notes to match a vocalist's inflection, but by adding certain notes—the so-called "blue notes"—to the major scale, a dissonance is created that is immediately identifiable as sounding "blue."

# How Blues Scales Are Made

Musicians playing the blues have a vast collection of notes to use in their improvisations and compositions—most of the notes of the major scale, the associated blue notes, and notes in other scales that complement other chords being played. It's also perfectly acceptable to add chromatic notes for color. Taken together, this adds up to far too many choices for a beginning improviser. The blues scale is a sort of distillation—it contains notes that are almost guaranteed to sound good when improvising and jamming. As players become more advanced, they can start adding other notes to get different, more complex sounds. But for beginning improvisers, the blues scale is an excellent foundation.

Musicians usually think about the blues scale in relation to the major scale with which it is associated. The basic blues scale contains the root note of the scale, the minor third, the fourth, the augmented fourth, the fifth, and the flatted seventh.

**THEORY AND PRACTICE**

Before you start confusing diminished chords with augmented chords (and calling them demented), here's a rundown:

- *Minor intervals:* The second, third, sixth, or seventh is lowered by half a step; these can also be called "flatted."
- *Augmented intervals:* The fourth or fifth is raised by half a step.
- *Diminished intervals:* The fourth or the fifth is lowered by half a step.
- *Perfect intervals:* Usually refer to fourths, fifths, and octaves.

 **Track 27, Example 1**

C Major          C Blues

Now let's look at how to find the blues scale in the more complex key of A Major. To find the blues scale, start with the root (A), omit the second, play a flatted third (C♮ instead of C♯), play the fourth (D), play a sharp fourth (D♯), play the fifth (E), omit the sixth, and play a flatted seventh (G♮ instead of G♯).

A Major          A Blues

# Learning the Blues Scales

The blues scale has an almost instantly identifiable sound, so it's easy to find by ear. But finding does not mean learning. A good way to internalize the notes of the blues scale is to practice them in small, repeated chunks.

For example, let's go back to C Major. Start with the first three notes. It's useful to anchor these right-hand melody notes with the underlying harmony, so play the major chord of the scale with the left hand while experimenting with right-hand sounds. You can start by playing the following riff. Once you've learned these three notes, improvise using those same three notes. As always, all practice—including improvising—should be done in strict time. With these exercises, playing with a metronome clicking in the background at about 100 beats per minute is a good idea. Listen to the recorded example, which starts with a three-note riff, then a four-note riff, then five, then six, then the full blues scale, and then the scale running up and down the keyboard. The steps for learning how to do this are broken down in these written examples. For each riff, first play the notes as written, and then noodle around using just those notes.

In the first two measures, play only three notes. (You can start with what's written, but don't be afraid to noodle around on your own.) Then play two measures using four notes, then five notes, and then all six notes.

 **Track 28, Example 2**

When you are comfortable playing the six-note scale, it's time to break it out and play it using notes all over the keyboard in various combinations and rhythms. Start by playing adjacent notes in the scale. Then as you gain confidence, start skipping notes, repeating notes, and jumping around the keyboard. The recorded example (Example 2) contains a sample improvisation used to get comfortable with the blues scale.

> **SOUR NOTES**
>
> Beginning blues players often become enamored with the blues scales, overusing them as they run up and down the keyboard. It sounds impressive, yes, but to listeners already familiar with the blues language, simply running scales all over the piano gets boring very quickly.
>
> As soon as you are comfortable with the notes in the blues scale, start experimenting with different melodic shapes, riffs, and rhythms to add musical interest to your growing virtuosity.

There are numerous ways to finger the blues scales. Because players will start and stop and turn around on different notes, there isn't just one fingering that works. It's always more effective, however, to get started with a consistent fingering, so here are some examples of workable fingerings.

Note that the basic rules are the same for major and minor scales:

- The basic chromatic scale patterns of using the third finger on black notes and the thumb on white notes is a good starting point because blues scales tend to have a lot of alternating white-note-black-note sequences.

- Avoid putting the thumb on a black note.

- Avoid playing with the pinky unless you are at the top note of your phrase.

- The smoothest way to transition from one set of notes to another is to pass the thumb under the third and fourth finger, or to pass the third or fourth finger over the thumb. If necessary, this passing movement can always be done with the second finger.

- Avoid trying to pass one finger over another.

# Putting It All Together

A traditional blues tune follows a fairly set format. As always with music, there are many exceptions and variations. But thousands upon thousands of blues songs have been composed using the same basic format, and it's a good place to practice blues scales over the fundamental harmonies so often used in songs.

The basic blues tune uses three chords. Any guess as to which ones? The I, the IV, and the V, just like you learned in Chapter 7. So a good way to practice the blues scales is to use them in the groups you'll most often find them in a real song.

The following groups of chords are common blues keys. Practice the blues scales in these groups to get used to how they are most commonly used in songs.

In each of the following exercises, first play the chords and scales as written. Then instead of playing a scale, try improvising as you move from chord to chord, as demonstrated in the recording. (Note that the recording contains an improvisation, which is not written out: you are supposed to make up your own.)

**Track 29, Example 3**

C, F, and G

A, D, and E

*continues*

*continued*

**B♭, E♭, and F**

**E♭, A♭, and B♭**

## Rhythm and Form in the Blues

You're just moments away from playing and turning these exercises into full-fledged blues tunes. What's left is to understand the form and rhythmic organization of the blues.

**THEORY AND PRACTICE**

We've been referring to the I, the IV, and the V chord in this chapter, but to be technically correct, we need to add a flatted seventh to each of these to get a real blues sound. The flatted seventh is the note that is one full step down from the name of the chord. So a C7 chord includes the notes of the C chord, plus the note that is one full step down from C: B♭. The F7 chord includes the notes of the F chord, plus an E♭. The G7 chord includes the notes of the G chord, plus an F. You'll hear the sounds of the seventh when you practice the blues shuffle.

The 12-bar blues form is the most basic (and the most common) incarnation of the blues. There are many other variations of the blues, but master this one first, and you can sit in on a blues jam.

The basic blues form has 12 measures in it, divided into three lines, each containing four measures.

- The first four bars are played using the I chord.

- The second line starts with two bars of the IV chord followed by two bars of the I chord.

- The third line contains a bar of the V chord, a bar of the IV chord, and a bar of the I chord.

Start with the simple left-hand shuffle pattern you learned in Chapter 7. You'll immediately hear how familiar this sounds because the basic 12-bar blues pattern is the foundation of so much popular music.

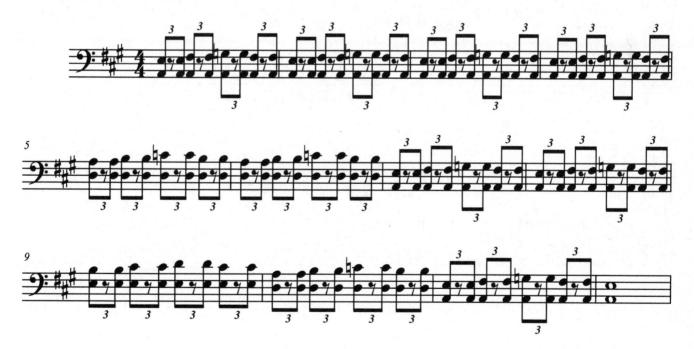

## Turning Blues Patterns into Blues Music

Now let's see how we can turn exercises and patterns into music. A common technique in the blues is call and response. For the solo pianist, this technique can be applied by having the left hand do something complicated while the right hand is doing something simple, and vice versa.

Start with the left-hand shuffle pattern in the key of A, and alternate it with a right-hand melodic pattern that uses the blues scales of A, D, and E. When you practice this exercise, use the written example as a model. Then break out and do your own thing. This is your chance to use the blues scale to play whatever you want.

**Track 30, Example 4**

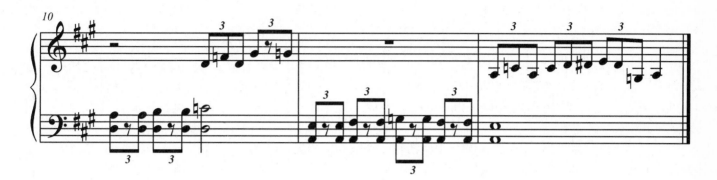

Here is a list of the basic blues chords (the I, IV, and V chords) in all 12 keys:

- C–F–G
- G–C–D
- D–G–A
- A–D–E
- E–A–B
- B–E–F♯
- F♯–B–C♯
- D♭–G♭–A♭
- A♭–D♭–E♭
- E♭–A–B♭
- B♭–E♭–F
- F–B♭–C

Now you're ready to try to create your own blues by using any of the scales you've learned in any of the keys. Practice one scale at a time—and have fun.

## The Least You Need to Know

- The blues scale can be used to improvise, create riffs, and supply melodic material.
- The blues scale consists of the first note of the major scale, the flatted third, the fourth, the sharp fourth, the fifth, and the flat seventh.
- There is no formal fingering.
- The 12-bar blues form is a basic pattern that forms the backbone of thousands of blues songs.
- Blues can be improvised by playing notes from the blues scales over the chords in the blues progression.

**Chapter**

# 12

# Good Grief, More Scales

## In This Chapter

- Fingering and practicing chromatic scales
- Fingering and practicing whole-tone scales
- Improvising exercises for whole-tone scales
- Pentatonic scales

So far, we've learned 12 major scales, 36 minor scales (12 keys times three different types of minor scales), and an additional 60 modes. We've also learned 12 blues scales.

But we're not done yet.

The study of scales can actually take a whole book, just by itself. There are endless variations on the modes, many of which are used in the music of non-Western cultures, as well as in jazz or experimental art music. A complete catalogue of all the possible scales and modes is beyond the scope of this book. We will, however, introduce a few more scales that are widely used in both classical and jazz music, as well as exercises for practicing.

## Chromatic Scales

One of the most important scale patterns is the chromatic scale. The chromatic scale contains every single note—all the black notes and all the white notes. Indeed, you can start it on the very lowest note of the piano and go all the way up to the highest note on the piano, playing all 88 keys.

**FLYING FINGERS**

The following tips will help you learn the chromatic scale:

- The fingers should play the notes close to the middle of the white keys and the ends of the black keys. The fingers should be well-rounded.
- Long fingernails will make this scale more difficult to play.
- Fingers should move from the knuckle joint with minimum wrist movement.
- Practice at mezzo forte (medium-loud).
- Start by learning the ascending right hand, and then the descending left hand.
- Only when the foregoing patterns are mastered, start the descending right hand and ascending left hand.
- Practice starting from any note on the piano.

The chromatic scale is an important piano technique to master, because it is used by so many composers in so many different instances—in delicate runs, in crashing bravura passages, and in everything in between. Practicing the chromatic scale teaches speed; it also reinforces the thumb-under/fingers-over scale technique.

## Fingering and Practicing the Chromatic Scales

As with other scales, note that there are several ways of fingering chromatic scales. The most common approach for right-hand ascending and left-hand descending is as follows:

- The third finger always plays on the black notes.

- The thumb passes under the third finger to play the white notes.

- When you arrive at a pair of white notes (B and C; F and E), the first white note is played with the thumb, and the second white note is played with the second finger, after which the 3–1–3–1 fingering pattern resumes.

When the right hand is descending and the left hand is ascending, follow these fingering rules:

- The third finger passes over the thumb to play the black notes.

- The thumb plays the white notes.

- When the pianist arrives at the groups of two white notes, the first white note is played with the second finger and the second white note is played with the thumb, after which the 3–1–3–1 fingering pattern resumes.

The following exercises are designed to get you playing the chromatic scales in time, while doing something else with the other hand—in this case, working your way through the basic triads (three-note chords) in all keys. Two exercises—scales and chords—all for the practice of one.

Track 31, Example 1

## Playing Hands Together in Contrary Motion

Starting with both thumbs on D, the left hand descends while the right hand ascends. This is actually much easier than it looks, and may be easier than practicing hands apart because the two hands are exact mirror images of each other. They play exactly the same fingers, which helps reinforce the fingering pattern. Play the pattern until each hand reaches the next D note with the thumb.

Playing in the opposite direction (the right-hand-descending/left-hand-ascending approach) is a little trickier because it requires you to remember that every time you reach the end of a series of black keys, you must put the second finger on the following white key (not the thumb). This takes a lot of repetition, because it seems intuitive to simply pass the thumb under. The problem with playing intuitively is that there are no fingers left for the following white note. Thus, the fingering for this direction is as follows:

 **Track 32a, Example 2**

## Chromatic Scales in Parallel Motion

Playing chromatic scales in parallel motion (in which the hands go up or down the scale in the same direction at the same time) is much trickier.

The difficulty lies in dealing with the two white notes—the E and the F, and the B and the C. When one hand is playing the thumb and the second finger, the other hand has to play those two fingers in the opposite order.

 **Track 32b (0:09), Example 3**

The most effective way to practice this is to concentrate on the right hand when it is descending and the left hand when it is ascending. This is because it is easier to trust the ascending right hand and the descending left hand, which have fingerings that seem more natural and intuitive. With the descending right hand and the ascending left hand, the pianist needs to be sure that the second finger is placed correctly when the fingers reach the two-note white groups of B and C, and E and F.

Getting to the point where the correct fingering is automatic takes practice, but it is well worth it. Parallel chromatic scales can be used for great effect in improvisations. Composers often use this technique. Additionally, practicing this technique teaches you how to use your hands independently.

**THEORY AND PRACTICE**

You might notice that notes in the chromatic scale are "spelled" (musician talk for "written") with sharps going up the scale and flats going down. This is a convention, not a rule, but composers tend to follow it unless they are going every which way up and down. In that case, they write using the way that seems to make the most sense for reading and expediency.

Spelling the same note (say, an F♯ and a G♭) two different ways is called "enharmonic" spelling, and is generally done to conform to music theory rules or to make reading easier for the performer.

# Whole-Tone Scales

Whole-tone scales are the same idea as chromatic scales, but instead of going up the piano in half steps, they go up in whole steps—for instance, from C to D to E to F♯. They are not used as commonly as chromatic scales.

The whole-tone scale sounds a little unsettled and spacey, and was used by Impressionist composers like Claude Debussy. In the whole-tone scale, the distance between each note is always one full step. There are no half steps, or leading tones, which seem to push the scale to a resting point.

There are only two different whole-tone scales, although they can start on any key. The first group includes the notes C, D, E, F♯, G♯, and A♯; the second group contains C♯, D♯, F, G, A, and B.

W.T. scale starting on C          W. T. scale starting on C#

**FLYING FINGERS**

You can make learning the whole-tone scale easier if you divide the notes in an octave into two clusters: the cluster of white and black notes from C to E, and the cluster of white and black notes from F to B.

The whole-tone scale starting on C plays only the white notes in the first cluster group (C–D–E), and only the black notes in the second cluster (F♯, G♯, A♯).

The whole-tone scale starting on F plays only the white notes in the first cluster, and only the black notes in the second cluster.

Once you've gotten used to these patterns, see if you can play a whole-tone scale starting on any note.

Practice whole-tone scales with left-hand chords. You'll notice that whole-tone scales can't be played with basic triads without sounding terribly dissonant. They can, however, be played with some more complex chords, many of which are commonly found in jazz.

Practice playing the first group of whole-tone scales (C–D–E–F♯–G♯–A♯) over the following chords, and then go ahead and improvise using the first group of whole-tone scales over these chords.

**Track 33a, Example 4**

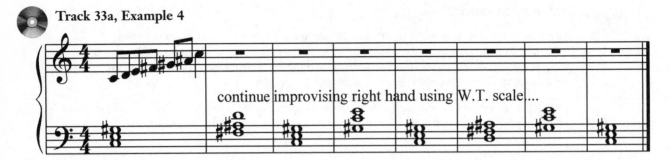

Practice playing the second group of whole-tone scales over the following chords, and then go ahead and improvise using the second group of whole-tone scales.

**Track 33b (0:26), Example 5**

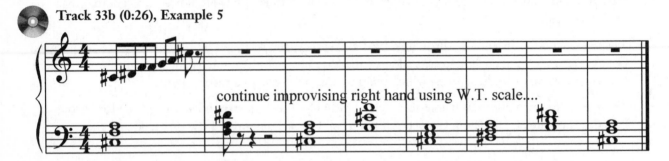

# Major and Minor Pentatonic

There's one more scale you're going to want to know about, if only because you hear it practically every time you hear a rock-and-roll guitar solo. It's the pentatonic scale (not to be confused with the penta-scales discussed in Chapters 4 and 5). The pentatonic scale is used in folk music throughout the world, and it is much beloved by guitarists because of the way the fretboard is organized. They can play solos in any key using the same fingering.

For pianists, the pentatonic scale is not such an iconic foundation scale, but it offers a safety net for beginning improvisers, or for band players who are trying to improvise on the fly. You know those people who can seemingly sit in and play along with a song they've never heard before? Often, they are using the pentatonic scale, which practically promises that they won't hit anything that sounds too awful. It's a great safety net scale.

There are two kinds of pentatonic scales: major and minor.

- The major pentatonic scale contains the first, second, third, fifth, and sixth notes of the major scale. (These are the first notes of the bass line of the Motown classic "My Girl"). You'll notice that the sound of the major pentatonic scale can vary greatly, from the sound of a Japanese song to an Irish folk tune, depending on where you start and end it.

- The minor pentatonic scale is the same as the blues scale, except that it doesn't have the jarring, bluesy augmented fourth. So using the notes of the major scale as a base, the minor pentatonic scale contains the first note, the flatted third, the fourth, the fifth, and the flatted seventh.

Here are the major and minor pentatonic scales in the key of C.

**Track 34, Example 6**

First learn the scales. Then use them to improvise over the primary chords. There's no sheet music for this one: it's a simple improvisation over the C, D, C, G, and C chords. In the recorded example, the right hand first uses the C Major pentatonic scale, but doesn't move around too much. In the second pass through the chord sequence, the right hand moves a little more freely.

When you've gotten the hang of the C Major and minor pentatonic scales, start your journey around all the keys, as always concentrating on the easier keys and the keys you are most likely to use if you are playing with a group.

## The Least You Need to Know

- To develop speed and fluency, learn the standard chromatic scale fingerings first; you can make changes, as required by individual pieces of music.
- Whole-tone scales sound spacey and unsettling, and are often played with altered or jazz chords.
- Diminished scales proceed up and down the keyboard in a pattern of alternating half steps and steps.
- The major and minor pentatonic scales are scales that fit easily over a wide range of chords and can be used to improvise.

# Practice Skills

## Part 4

They say that practice makes perfect, but the truth is that practice makes permanent: only perfect practice makes permanently perfect. The exercises in this chapter focus on practice skills, starting with using rhythm to help you sharpen your game and stay in the groove.

You'll also get more fingering and technique tips for technically challenging pieces, as well as exercises to develop hand independence (especially in the important area of controlling dynamics). We end by revisiting the iconic Charles Louis Hanon and learning how to adapt his exercises to work on transposing and chords.

# I've Got Rhythm

### In This Chapter

- Learning to practice with a metronome
- Understanding tempo and beats
- Using the metronome to develop improvisation fluency
- Using creative rhythm practice to solve technical problems

As the old song goes, if you've got rhythm, you've got music … or, put another way, if you don't have rhythm, you won't have music.

Like a human, music has a beating heart—a pulse, if you will. Everything in music takes place within the framework of time. We've already talked about the benefit of practicing exercises in rhythm. In this chapter, we focus on improving rhythm-related practice techniques.

Simply put, playing exercises—scales, improvisation exercises, chords, written music, patterns, and drills—in time is the best way to get the biggest bang for your practice buck.

Unfortunately, it's not always easy to keep perfect time while learning something that is technically tricky. You probably find yourself automatically slowing down when the next chord change is difficult, or when the fingering of the minor melodic scale gets flakey. Forcing yourself to practice in time—to not only get where you're supposed to go, but also to arrive there in time—ups the challenge. It also ups the rewards.

Practicing with a metronome and using creative rhythm variations can raise the bar a bit because practicing this way reveals weak spots. By not allowing yourself to slow down, you can overcome technical difficulties.

## The Metronome: Your New Best Friend

The metronome is a practice tool that is equally loathed and lauded by music students. Used thoughtfully and creatively, it can be your number one ally, not only in helping you control tempo and rhythm, but also in developing technical proficiency.

At its simplest, the metronome is nothing more than the world's most boring drummer, reliably banging out a steady series of unvarying beats. Being able to play with a metronome is your first step toward being able to play with others. The metronome also helps solo performers play with a sense of groove, or rhythmic pulse.

## Mechanical Metronomes

The mechanical metronome is a simple wind-up device that hasn't changed since its invention by Johann Nepomuk Mälzel in 1816. A weighted pendulum swings back and forth, clicking like the pendulum on a clock. An adjustable weight determines the speed, which is notated as *M.M.* The higher the weight sits on the pendulum, the slower the metronome ticks (as noted by numbers etched into the pendulum). The lower the weight, the faster the metronome ticks.

**UNIVERSAL LANGUAGE**

The symbol **M.M.** stands for Mälzel's Metronome and indicates the speed. The abbreviation M.M. is usually followed by a type of note, such as a quarter note, a dotted quarter note, or a half note. That is the note that gets the beat. The number that follows the note tells you how many of those notes are to be played in a minute. So the abbreviation M.M. might be followed with a quarter note and the number 108, which tells you that the quarter note gets the beat, and the piece is to be played at a moderate tempo, with 108 beats per minute.

## Digital Metronomes

Digital metronomes are inexpensive, portable, and often include features such as tuners (not especially useful for pianists, but very useful for guitarists, violinists, and others who need to tune their own instruments).

The digital metronome may include other features, such as flashing lights, the ability to click uneven swing beats, volume control, sound choices for the clicks, and more complex renderings of compound time, such as making a different noise on each downbeat. Metronomes are also built into digital pianos.

**SOUR NOTES**

Don't overcomplicate the issue of which metronome to buy! Many of the fanciest features work better in theory than in practice. For example, some models make a different sound on the downbeat of each measure. This sounds like a good idea, until you do heavy duty technical practice, at which time, you may get tired of waiting for the downbeat to come around so that you can restart a tricky passage. Similarly, having a flashing light is not a pedagogically useful device, as the pulse of the music needs to be sensed in advance, not reacted to after the fact. A common complaint with digital models is that the sound is unpleasant. So forget about fancy features and get a metronome with a sound you can live with—then, use it.

# How to Practice with a Metronome

The most obvious use for a metronome is to set the tempo, or speed. Composers have different ways of indicating the preferred speed of a piece of music. The first and most general indication is the style of a piece; even without tempo indications, musicians know the difference between a funeral march, a waltz, and a scherzo.

Beyond style, composers may give an indication such as lento (slow) or allegro (fast). Note, however, that these indications are subjective, and may mean different things to different composers and performers.

Finally, some composers use metronome markings, either giving a specific tempo or a range of tempi. Editors, too, may insert these markings in a score. Keep in mind that any metronome speeds from the Baroque and early Classical periods were not put there by the composers. The metronome hadn't yet been invented.

**UNIVERSAL LANGUAGE**

English may be the language of business, French may be the language of love, but Italian is the language of music. Pieces are played allegro and lento, largo and prestissimo, and everything in between. While there is no firm and inviolable correlation between a tempo marking and a specific metronome speed, the following guidelines can be used as a starting point:

- Largo: 40–60
- Larghetto: 60–66
- Adagio: 66–76
- Andante: 76–108
- Moderato: 108–120
- Allegro: 120–168
- Presto: 168–200
- Prestissimo: 200 and up

Beyond setting the speed, the metronome helps the player maintain that speed. Beginning musicians are often shocked at how the metronome seems to speed up (during the hard parts of the music, of course) and slow down (during the easy parts). Obviously, the metronome is doing nothing of the kind: it is all a matter of perception. It's the musician who is slowing down or speeding up. As a musician, you have to be able to maintain a steady tempo throughout the piece even though your perception of speed may change depending on the character of the music, the technical demands, the dynamics and density, and even the emotional flow.

Of course, sometimes tempo changes are part of the music. Classical music, in particular, relies heavily on the expressive devices of *ritardando* (getting slower) and *accelerando* (getting faster). For classical musicians, the metronome is only part of the journey. Musicians must be able to play in an even, consistent tempo. But they also must develop the musical sensibility to learn how to vary that tempo when appropriate.

**FLYING FINGERS**

Here are some tips for playing with the metronome:

- Listen before you play.
- Count off the beats in your head. You need to actually feel the pulse before you start playing.
- Count the subdivisions if the piece has them (one-and-two-and …).
- Imagine the first few bars of the music, and how they will sound with the metronome.

To get used to playing with the metronome, start with a simple scale. Set the metronome at a speed you can achieve, and then increase it as you gain fluency. In the recorded example, the metronome is set at 80. Play the first two measures until you feel secure playing on the beat. Then try the next two measures (two eighth notes to a beat); add the remaining measures, which contain three notes to a beat and four notes to a beat, respectively.

 **Track 35, Example 1**

In the following piece by William Duncombe, an English classical composer, the quarter note gets the beat. In the first two measures, the beat is divided into triplets. In the third and fourth measures, the beat is divided into even eighth notes. Only the music for the right hand is included because the purpose of this example is to play the varying rhythm with the metronome, not to worry about learning and adding left-hand notes.

 **Track 36, Example 2**

M.M. ♩ = 80

To learn to play with the metronome, start with simple scale patterns. Once you are confident playing scales with the metronome, try playing some pieces with the metronome. Choose music at a medium tempo (between M.M. = 72 and M.M. = 112) and pieces that you already know well so that you can concentrate on staying with the metronome.

## Practicing Improvisation with the Metronome

The metronome also can be used to practice improvisation. Take the C blues scale you learned in Chapter 11, and see how using the metronome can help you develop both fluency and groove. The following exercise is played in straight eighths; in the recorded example, the metronome is set at M.M. = 84. You can choose your own speed, depending on your comfort level.

The first part of the exercise is simply the blues scale played with the metronome. In the second part of the example, the performer improvises using the notes of the blues scale. In this exercise, the beginning of the improvisation is written out. The recorded example continues with some improvisatory ideas that are not written out. The point of this exercise is not to play exactly what is on the recording, nor to learn some sheet music. Rather, you are learning to use the material of the C blues scale to create your own improvisation in time with the metronome.

**Track 37a, Example 3**

Now try moving on to swing. The next example starts by playing the scale in swing triplets, with the metronome set at 84. In the second part of the exercise, the player improvises using triplets. The first part of the improvisation is written out in the example. Then the player continues improvising, using swing rhythm, with syncopated stops. When listening to the recorded example, listen to how the metronome keeps ticking away in the background.

**Track 37b (0:48), Example 4**

## Using the Metronome to Practice Chords

Good improvisation skills also require facility with chords. Look at some metronome exercises that can help develop chord fluency. Keep in mind, any of the chord exercises in Chapters 5 and 7 also can be practiced with the metronome.

Consider the ii–V–I series (used extensively in all kinds of jazz) and run it through the circle of fifths. It's enormously valuable to be able to play a series of chords in time. If you're already fluent in playing chords, don't feel left out. There are plenty of ways to raise the difficulty of these exercises to challenge your playing skill. For example, try adding sevenths, or speeding up the tempo.

Being able to play your basic chord progressions with the metronome means that you won't have to figure out the chords when reading a lead sheet or comping chords in a jazz trio. That leaves you free to concentrate on your groove and your leads.

# The Metronome and Technique

Some passages are just plain difficult to play. You've probably had the experience of being able to play most of a piece of music, but always seeming to make the same mistake in the same place. You may have tried playing the section faster, slower, and hands apart—yet still, when you approach it, you do so with uncertainty.

To avoid this pitfall, approach new pieces methodically:

- Don't rush.

- Use correct, consistent fingering.

- Practice carefully, in small sections.

- Practice one hand at a time (if it makes musical sense to do so).

At this stage, the goal is to play the piece correctly—at any tempo, no matter how slow.

Once you have learned the piece so that you can play it well at a slow speed, it's time to use the metronome to increase speed. Follow these tips to get yourself playing a piece at its intended tempo:

- Play the piece with the metronome at a slow tempo. Note any rough spots. If necessary, turn off the metronome and work on them in isolation until you can play them smoothly.

- Try again with the metronome.

- When you can play the section of music three times in a row with no mistakes, raise the speed a notch on a mechanical metronome, or three to four beats per minute on a digital metronome.

- Play correctly three times, raise the tempo, and repeat.

- When you start noticing that the speed seems uncomfortably fast, stop. This is when you start making mistakes. Go down a few notches in speed, and start the process all over again.

## Using Rhythmic Variation

Another technique that can be applied using the metronome is rhythmic variation. By varying the rhythm in several different ways (which means playing incorrect rhythms, or—perhaps more accurately—rhythms the composer didn't actually write), a musician may be able to teach his fingers several different ways to approach the problem. This can also be an effective way to fix a chronic mistake, because it takes it out of context of the original mistake.

The easiest way to apply rhythmic variation to a fast passage of even notes is to change the rhythm so that instead of playing a series of even notes, you are alternating long notes with short notes or short notes with long notes. Try it with the following scale. Your goal is to play the scale, in eighth notes, at M.M. = 100 (100 quarter notes per minute). More advanced players can use this exercise with two-handed scales, more difficult scales, faster tempi—or all three.

 **Track 38, Example 5**

♩ = 120

*continues*

*continued*

To see how this technique can be applied to learning a piece of music, look at Muzio Clementi's famous intermediate-level "Sonatina in C Major, Opus 36, No. 1." In the last beat of measure 6, and in measures 7 and 8 (the last two measures of this segment), there is a section that often trips up students.

**Track 39a, Example 6**

To learn this section, first be sure you have the fingering correct. These notes are supposed to be played fairly quickly, but start by learning it at a slow speed—perhaps M.M. = 72 (72 half notes per minute, because we are in cut time). Once you've learned the basic sequence with the correct fingering, try practicing it using the two rhythmic variations presented in the next example. Then try the piece with its normal rhythms at successively faster tempos, until you arrive at your goal (somewhere around 100). The recorded example includes a practice tempo and practice rhythms.

**Track 39b (0:15), Example 7**

The technique of rhythmic variation can be applied to many fast passages, and is especially effective in passages using scale patterns. It requires your fingers to move very quickly on every other note—faster than they will actually have to move when playing the piece in correct time. When you put it back together in the correct (and easier) rhythm, your fingers will actually have an easier job.

## More Rhythmic Variation

Another way to work on difficult passages is to break them down into smaller sections, with added beats that aren't in the music.

For example, look at the series of chords in the next example. Assume that we want to play these at a tempo of M.M. = 92. But there's a bit of jumping around that makes this a challenge. As always, more advanced players can substitute bigger jumps, progressions in more difficult keys, or faster tempi.

At first, it may be too difficult to play the entire series of these chords in time. Going slowly in sections is one solution, but you can also break up the entire progression into smaller rhythmic units. Notice that in the first pass through the series, we start at half speed (by playing half notes, not quarter notes). In the following variations, there is a lot of time to rest between moves. The resting time gets shorter and shorter. Finally, try the series at the intended speed.

**Track 40, Example 8**

The same strategy can be applied to any piece that is giving you difficulty. Whether you use rhythmic variation or planned resting points, the key in creative rhythm practice is to stay in time (preferably with a metronome). By forcing yourself to practice in strict rhythm, you refuse to allow difficult spots to slow you down or to become consistent trouble spots.

## The Least You Need to Know

- Metronomes can be used to help develop a good sense of rhythm and speed.
- Metronomes can be used to help pianists solve technical problems.
- All exercises and technical practice should be done in strict rhythm.
- Increasing tempo, rhythmic variation, and creative repetition can be used to learn technically difficult pieces.

# Expressive Exercises

## In This Chapter

- Exercises to develop dynamic control
- Learning about articulation
- Techniques for better control and phrasing
- Using the piano pedals

When you think about piano exercises, the first thing that usually comes to mind is technique. Developing the ability to play the right notes smoothly and fluently in time is fundamental, of course. But for as much time as you spend working on technique and accuracy, there is more to music than mere notes.

After all, with today's technology, a computer can play notes and rhythms more correctly, consistently, and precisely than any concert pianist. What the pianist brings to the process is interpretation, expression, and artistry. These aspects of playing require not only control, but also the ability to realize an emotional goal through technical means. Pianists create their own alchemy: they turn notes into music. In this chapter, we look at some exercises to develop control over expressive elements such as dynamics, articulation, and pedaling.

## Louds and Softs

To influence the mood and character of a piece of music, the pianist's most obvious tool is the use of dynamics. Dynamics can be defined as louds, softs, and everything in between.

To get a sense of dynamics over the whole range of the piano, play the following exercise. Try it at different tempos—perhaps M.M. = 60, 80, and 100—to get a sense of the interplay between dynamics and speed. Try experimenting with and without the pedal as well.

**Track 41, Example 1**

## Crescendos and Decrescendos

Using dynamics is more than a question of how loudly a passage is played. There is also the matter of changing from one volume to another. Is the change sudden and dramatic, like the famous crash in Haydn's "Surprise Symphony"? Or is it subtle and gradual? Does the sound build by volume alone? Or is it by the addition of more notes, thicker chords, and crashing bass notes? Does it quietly echo what has gone before? Where is its climax point? How does the use of dynamics build to the climax? What happens after it?

An important function of dynamics is to take the listener on an emotional musical journey. The energy of a piece of music has an ebb and flow that is determined by speed, volume, and changes in dynamics. The climax of a phrase is often found at its highest note. Playing a crescendo up to the high point of the phrase builds tension and excitement, which can then be released after the top of the phrase. This is a powerful dynamics technique that should be used with subtlety.

Typically, phrases tend to build as they rise in pitch, and recede as they lower in pitch. For example, look at this simple arpeggio pattern. In the recorded example, you'll hear an arpeggio played two ways. In the first example, the crescendo and decrescendo are used, if not incorrectly, then certainly in unusual places. The second example shows the more typical arc of dynamics rising and falling with the pitch of the phrase.

**Track 42, Example 2**

Sometimes, however, a rising passage is accompanied by a long descrescendo. In his piano sonatas, Mozart frequently brings a long chromatic scale up to a high note. Played with a long decrescendo at the very end, with a slight ritardando, the scale seems to rise to its inevitable resting point. Try practicing the following long chromatic scale as a gradual decrescendo. This passage is taken from Mozart's "Fantasie in D minor, K. 397."

**Track 43, Example 3**

**UNIVERSAL LANGUAGE**

More Italian lessons for musicians! Most commonly, dynamics are indicated using the traditional Italian terminology and abbreviations. From softest to loudest, they are as follows:

- Pianissimo (pp)
- Piano (p)
- Mezzopiano (mp)
- Mezzoforte (mf)
- Forte (f)
- Fortissimo (ff)

In addition, here are some other common terms:

- Szforsando (sf)—suddenly loud
- Crescendo (cresc.)—getting louder
- Decrescendo (decresc.)—getting softer
- Diminuendo (dim.)—getting softer

## Accents

Accents can be considered tiny sforzandos over individual notes or chords. Accents indicate that the note should be played louder than the surrounding notes. How much louder depends on the context: the accent is always played in reference to the overall dynamics, unless the composer's intention is to really rocket the listener off his seat.

Accents also can change the flow and sense of the music. To see how, try playing the following exercise as you normally would (which probably means stressing the downbeats and the strong beats a bit). Now try playing the same notes but with accents on different notes of the scale. It completely changes the feel.

**Track 44, Example 4**

Accents are frequently used in syncopated music, in which the stress is on a note that does not fall on a strong beat.

# Articulation

Dynamics are concerned with the volume of the sound; articulation is concerned with sound quality, and is a crucial component of that mysterious element called tone quality. Articulation and dynamics are close cousins, closely intertwined with creating the emotional feel of the music.

## Legato Touch

Legato, based on the Italian word "to tie," means to link notes together so that there is no break in sound between one note and the next. We do this by holding the first note down until the second note is played, then quickly releasing the first note. Legato is an important technique, used in singing passages. In the following exercise, the holding down motion is exaggerated to get used to the feel of holding down the first note while striking the second one.

**Track 45, Example 5**

Pairs of notes and chords can also be played legato. Note that sometimes, creative fingering, such as putting one finger over another, is required to achieve the legato. In the following example, hold down the thumb while connecting the top notes.

**Track 46a, Example 6**

continue same fingering

*continues*

*continued*
*10*

It is usually not possible to play a three-note chord and connect all of its three notes with those of another, subsequent three-note chord. (You would need six fingers for that feat.) In the right hand, the upper voice or voices will often be fingered so that they can be played legato, leaving the thumb to connect as best it can. The opposite is often true in the left hand. Or, as in the following example, fingers can "walk" over each other while notes that will connect easily are held by the other fingers. For instance, in the right hand, on the first chord, hold the thumb while the other fingers move to the new position.

 **Track 46b (0:43), Example 7**

> **THEORY AND PRACTICE**
>
> The subject of tone quality is of endless fascination to pianists. You understand the mechanics of your instrument: sound is produced by the strike of a felted hammer against a string. You also understand that regardless of your gestures, you can only change one aspect about how a string is struck: the velocity of the hammer hitting and releasing the string. You know that there is nothing the pianist can do to change the tone of that sound after she has depressed a key. Yet nonetheless, different pianists can create very different and identifiable tones on the same instrument. You can't explain exactly how one does this—but somehow, by combining dynamics, articulation, pedaling, legato, and other expressive techniques, you can create your own sound.

## Staccato

Staccato is the opposite of legato. It sounds a bit like the pianist touched a hot stove and removed her fingers as quickly as possible. Staccatos can be quick and light, or dramatic and strident. There are several different techniques for achieving different kinds of staccato sounds at different speeds and volumes.

Finger staccato is used for quick light passages, usually of single notes. In a finger staccato, the finger is raised from the knuckle joint. When playing sequences of staccato notes, strive for an even, controlled volume. The following example should initially be played with the right hand only. Beginners may want to ignore the left hand part. More advanced players should add the left hand, played legato, once they have mastered the right-hand fingering.

**Track 47a, Example 8**

Wrist staccato is more commonly used with double notes (such as passages in sixths), where the fingers stay fairly fixed while the wrist bounces.

**Track 47b (0:16), Example 9**

Arm staccato is used for bigger, crashing sounds, often in passages with big jumps. The following example combines wrist staccato for the faster eighth-note passages with arm staccato for the bigger jumps.

**Track 48, Example 10**

## Repeated Notes

Playing the same note over and over is a particular challenge, especially with a fast staccato. Changing fingers on fast repeated staccato notes can help avoid fatigue and create a more even and controlled sound. Changing fingers requires the finger that previously played the note to be completely off the key and out of the way, which helps to ensure a clean repetition. The finger change is generally achieved with the first, second, and third fingers, which alternate. The wrist moves slightly in a circular pattern.

This technique may be better practiced (at least at first) on a weighted electronic keyboard, because the keys are evenly weighted. On acoustic pianos, the speed of repetition can vary enormously from one instrument to another, from one part of the keyboard to another (lower notes are more heavily weighted than higher notes), and even from one note to its neighbor if the piano hasn't been regulated properly.

*continue staccatos and fingering*

## Slurs

Slurs combine legato and staccato to help shape short musical phrases. A typical slur will use legato touch to connect the first note to a second note, which is released more quickly, and may be played a shade quieter than the first note.

**Track 49, Example 11**

# Pedaling

Last, but certainly not least, pedals are in the pianist's arsenal of expressive tools.

The standard grand piano has three pedals: the left pedal, often called the quiet pedal or una corda; the middle pedal, called the sostenuto; and the right pedal, called the sustain.

## The Right Pedal

Of the three pedals, the right pedal is by far the most important and commonly used. Also called the sustain pedal, it lifts all the dampers of the piano at once, which allows all the strings to vibrate freely. This means that as long as the pedal is down (and the dampers are up), all the notes you play will continue to sound until they finally die away.

The sustain pedal also changes the tone of the piano. Piano strings vibrate in what is called "sympathy" with each other. Strings you didn't actually play will vibrate according to a mathematical relationship with the principal note, involving their vibrations per minute and the length of the strings. So when you play a low C with the sustain pedal depressed, all the notes with a harmonic relationship to that C will also vibrate, giving the tone a richer, fuller sound.

**THEORY AND PRACTICE**

To see how overtones (also called "harmonics") work, press down middle C without actually playing it. The damper of this one note will be up, allowing that string to ring. Now play a low C on the piano (play it hard, and let it up immediately). If the piano is in tune, you will hear the middle C ringing quietly, because its string is free to vibrate, and it responds in sympathy to the lower C being played. Each note has a series of notes that will vibrate this way. These extra vibrations are what give the piano its rich, full sound when the sustain pedal is depressed. This effect can only be achieved with an acoustic piano.

The main purpose of this pedal is to connect the sounds and layer them on top of each other. But too many sounds on top of each other sounds like a muddy mess. So the pedal has to be changed with changes in harmony, according to the style of the music and the artist's interpretation.

The basic technique for pedaling smoothly to create an uninterrupted sound is called syncopated pedaling. If you put your foot down when you play the note or chord, then raise the pedal when you raise your hand, then depress it again when you play the next note, the pedal won't hold the sound in between notes. The sound is jerky and awkward. In the next example, using the pedal holds the note exactly when the pianist's finger holds down the note; when the pianist releases the note, she releases the pedal, creating a clunky, disjointed sound.

Track 50a, Example 12

Instead, hold the pedal until after you have played the next chord. As soon as that next chord is played, hold the chord, and quickly release the pedal and put it back down again. This is shown in the pedal markings under the notes. The stylized "ped" indicates when to put down the pedal, while the circle icon indicates when the pedal should be released. This syncopating technique connects the sounds, but releases the old harmonies as soon as possible after the new harmony has been played. The goal is to NOT change the pedal in time with the music.

Practice tips:

- Start by playing the first chord and pedaling at the same time. Keep the pedal down.

- Continue to hold the pedal down while playing the second chord.

- While holding the second chord down, quickly release the pedal and put it down again.

- Release the chord, hold the pedal, and repeat the process with the next chord.

In the recorded example, you'll first hear the line of chords played correctly; in the second pass, the vocal track tells you where to hold the notes and where to hold and release the pedal.

**Track 50b (0:11), Example 13**

Practice the previous exercise until you automatically alternate playing and pedaling. It seems awkward at first, but this is one of those tricky-to-learn skills that becomes utterly commonplace in surprisingly little time.

## The Left Pedal

The quiet pedal, on the left, is the next most often used pedal, although it's used only a fraction of the time. On a grand piano, the pedal shifts the entire keyboard and the whole inside action of the piano so that the hammers are moved over. Instead of striking two strings, the hammers of the lower notes now strike only one string (hence the name "una corda"). In the treble notes, instead of striking three strings, the hammers only strike two strings.

As with the sustain pedal, the quiet pedal also affects the tone quality, because the part of the hammers that strike the string when the action is moved is a softer part of the hammer. This creates a muted tone, almost like the difference between hitting a drum with a wooden drum stick and a soft mallet.

On an upright piano, the una corda works differently than it does on a grand piano. Instead of shifting the piano's action, it moves the keys down perhaps a quarter of an inch closer to the keybed. This smaller distance means that you cannot play with as much force; hence the notes sound quieter. But there is no difference in tone quality. If you have an upright piano (or a digital piano with three pedals), however, it is still worth practicing with the left pedal simply to get used to the feel of playing while using your left foot, or even both feet at the same time.

To hear the difference between the normal action and the una corda, experiment with sound on a grand piano.

Play a series of chords slowly, at around M.M. = 60. Play deep into the keys with your fingertips, and then raise your wrist and pull your hand up from the keys in a sort of floating motion. Listen carefully to the sound, first with the normal piano action, and then with the una corda. Then repeat with the sustain pedal. (It takes some practice to get comfortable playing with two pedals at the same time.)

## The Middle Pedal

Last, and most definitely least, is the middle pedal. The middle pedal on an American upright either works as a practice mute with a layer of felt dropped between the hammers and the strings to create a dull, muted tone, or it works like a sustain pedal for the bass notes only. In Europe, most upright pianos don't even have a middle pedal.

On grand pianos, many middle pedals don't even work properly. When the middle pedal does work, it sustains only the notes that were played and held down immediately before the sustain pedal was pressed.

To see how this works, you need a grand piano. Play a bass octave. While still holding the notes, press the middle pedal. Those notes will continue to sound as long as you hold the middle pedal; other notes can be played, and they will sound as they normally do with no pedal.

The sostenuto pedal was developed in the late nineteenth century, long after the majority of the iconic classical and romantic works for piano were composed. So it's rarely used, except in Impressionistic music and some contemporary music.

## The Least You Need to Know

- Dynamics allow the pianist to exploit the range of sound possible on a piano for expressive purposes.
- Articulation refers to the way notes are played, and helps shape the music and bring it to life.
- Syncopated pedaling is the technique that allows pianists to maintain continuity of sound without sounding muddy.
- Dynamics, articulation, and pedaling are the elements of artistic expression that make each pianist's performance of a piece uniquely his own.

# One Brain, Two Hands

## In This Chapter

- Balancing dynamics to bring out the most important voice
- Bringing out right-hand and left-hand melodies
- Handling melodies that change hands
- Preparing to play canons and fugues

One of the reasons playing the piano is considered so good for neural development is that it requires the pianist to use both sides of the brain at once.

Pianists may play an accompaniment in one hand and a melody in the other, requiring them to balance the dynamics between the hands. The melody may shift between hands, alternating between the right hand and the left hand—having a musical conversation, so to speak. Or perhaps the notes are having a downright argument, with right and left hands playing two different things at the same time. This chapter offers practice techniques and exercises for developing hand independence.

# A Question of Balance

The solo pianist is responsible for supplying all the functions in a piece of music: melody, harmony, bass line, and rhythm. But not all of these functions are equal. It is up to the pianist, as interpreter, to decide how and when to bring out which parts.

## Balanced Dynamics

Typically, the pianist needs to bring out the melody, which is played most commonly (although certainly not always) with the right hand. Bringing out the melody while playing full chords in the left hand can be a challenge.

Start simply by playing an easy five-finger pattern with the right-hand forte and the left-hand piano.

Track 51a, Example 1

**THEORY AND PRACTICE**

Some digital keyboards have a split keyboard function, with which you can play the bass in one voice and the treble in another. Playing in two different voices helps you hear the different parts of a piece, and may affect how you choose to interpret them, even on a traditional acoustic piano. It's a new perspective that's worth exploring.

Once you've mastered playing the right hand loudly while playing the left hand quietly, you can try this technique with other exercises in this book, scales in particular.

Next, you need to be able to bring out a melody with the right hand while playing something different with the left hand. Try the melody you played above with an Alberti bass accompaniment. The melody should be played forte; the accompaniment should be played piano.

Track 51b (0:11), Example 2

It's not as common, but the left hand sometimes gets the melody. Try the same five-finger pattern exercise, but this time, bring out the left hand while playing quietly with the right hand.

Track 51c (0:24), Example 3

Finally, try an exercise in which you play the melody with the left hand and a basic accompaniment with the right hand.

**Track 51d (0:37), Example 4**

## Controlling Articulation

Similarly, pianists are often called upon to use one type of articulation in the right hand while the left hand does something entirely different. Start by playing our simple five-finger pattern, playing legato with the left hand and staccato with the right hand. Then switch so that you are playing staccato with the left hand while playing legato with the right hand.

This is a bit like one of those children's games in which you tap your head and rub your stomach at the same time. It gets easier with practice. When you start, exaggerate the motions of pressing down the note with your left hand while plucking it up in a bouncing staccato with your right hand.

**Track 51e (0:51), Example 5**

# Inner Voices and Hand Changes

The melody can also switch between hands. Sometimes a melody played in one hand will be echoed or answered by a melody in the other hand. In the following example, the echo should be quieter than the main theme in the right hand.

**Track 52, Example 6**

As you play the following example, try to imagine that the hands are having a conversation with each other. Perhaps the left hand is saying "I want you to mow the lawn today," and the right hand is answering "I'm going to do it tomorrow."

Track 53, Example 7

# Counterpoint

Counterpoint is one of the most difficult techniques to master because it requires well-developed hand independence. Essentially, counterpoint requires playing two (or more) different—although related— parts at the same time.

A simple canon, or round, is the easiest form of counterpoint. Think of a group of children singing "Frere Jacques" in parts. That's what the pianist has to do—except the pianist plays all the parts.

A *fugue* is a more complex, fully developed counterpoint, with motifs and themes altered and played in different variations and sequences. In the great fugues of the Baroque era, there may be four voices—to be played with only two hands. Often, the middle voices are divided between the hands.

**UNIVERSAL LANGUAGE**

A full-fledged **fugue** may be a sophisticated musical form, but its name harks back to its origins as a round, or canon: *fugue* comes from the Italian word for "to hunt" or "to chase," as the musical parts chase each other.

**Track 54, Example 8**

Try the following simple two-part fugue. You might want to start by learning each hand alone. But with fugues, part of the challenge is putting the hands together. Think of fugues as the ultimate musical multi-task: you may need to practice this piece one or two measures at a time until you get the hang of having different hands doing entirely different things.

## The Least You Need to Know

- Being able to vary the dynamics of each hand independently of one another gives pianists the ability to bring out different parts for expressive purposes.
- The melody is not always found in the right hand: sometimes it is found in the bass, and it also can be found in the middle voices, or be passed from one hand to the other.
- The two hands may be required to play different articulations (for example, legato in one hand and staccato in the other).
- Playing fugues requires being able to play with hand independence, and sometimes being able to play two voices with one hand.

# Advanced Fingering

## In This Chapter

- Learning to move smoothly from one position to another
- Learning techniques for cross-hand playing and hand-on-top-of-hand playing
- Learning and applying advanced fingering techniques
- Choosing alternate fingerings for ergonomic and artistic reasons

It bears repeating: playing the piano has a lot in common with athletics. As in any athletic activity, success is based on learning and perfecting a series of precise, practiced movements. For pianists, that means learning standard fingerings for common passages, and applying sound and consistent fingering principles to difficult technical passages. As pianists develop their skills, they learn that the basic patterns they practiced are malleable, and can be changed, altered, and adapted to fit any given situation. But first, the basics must be in place.

Advanced pianists learn standard fingerings and techniques. And then they learn to adapt. They learn what works best for them and for the particular piece of music. There are often several possible and workable fingerings for complex passages. But every fingering decision needs to take into account not only how to get *to* the note in question—but also how to get *from* it to the next one. So fingerings must be looked at in context of the phrase, the pianist's hand, and the musical and expressive demands of the piece.

## Practical Issues of Advanced Fingering

Playing the piano is in large measure a matter of getting from one place to another. And just like navigating using a road map, navigating on the keyboard is easier if you have a firm sense of where you are—and where you are going next.

You've probably noticed that different editions of the same piece of music often have very different fingerings added by editors. But all good fingerings help pianists connect the notes to achieve musical goals in the most ergonomic way possible. The challenge is what was ergonomic for the editor may not be ergonomic for the pianist. Some editors edit specifically for younger students and take small hand size as a given, which may require a different fingering when editing for adults.

**SOUR NOTES**

Don't be casual about fingering! It can't wait till later. How you finger a piece will affect whether and how you play it. It's important to deliberately choose a fingering, and then consistently apply the same fingering time after time.

## Continuity and Connections

One of the key ideas of fingering is making ergonomic connections between notes. Sometimes this requires solidly staying on the notes, with the hand in place, and using the current position as a starting point for moving to the next position. And sometimes it requires leaping up from the current note and using the momentum to propel the hand to its new position.

**FLYING FINGERS**

Always work on fingerings in phrases so you don't get stuck in the middle, one finger short of the final note. If a motif or pattern is repeated, check to see if there is one fingering that will work for each repetition. Sometimes there is, and sometimes—because of the placement of black notes—there isn't. But our brains like to see repeated patterns, so use them, if possible.

Whether you are physically connecting the notes and positions or flying from one place on the piano to another, the initial position is used as a launching pad for the new position. The goal is to create a sequence of motions that flow from one to the other. This is in contrast to what beginning piano students do: beginners usually play a note, take their finger off it, and then hover over the keys while looking for the next note. They don't play a phrase of music; they play a string of notes.

The advanced player knows that playing a series of notes means playing a series of linked movements. As your fingers learn the feeling of what they have to do to move, you no longer have to worry about finding notes, but can move seamlessly—which makes you free to concentrate on music, not notes.

Try a slightly more difficult variation of the scrunching-stretching exercises from Chapter 6.

Notice how, as you practice this pattern, your hand learns to contract and expand, using the note you have just played as a sort of navigation point for finding the next note. The technique of "constant contact" is an important one for moving securely in legato passages.

Now try the same exercise in the key of A♭. You will notice that the fingering has to change because of the different position of the white and black notes. Transposing this pattern into a variety of keys will yield big benefits in terms of teaching your hand to understand keyboard geography.

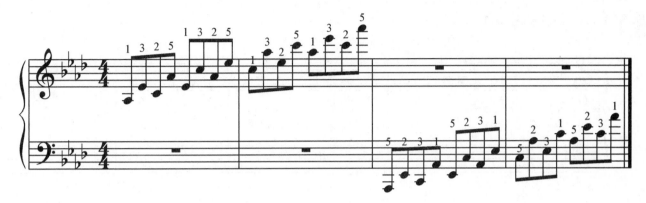

## Finger Substitutions

Sometimes, you run out of fingers before you run out of notes to play. In some cases, you can simply lift your hand and move it, but if a legato touch is called for, we need to find a way to connect the notes. Silently changing fingers on a note that is already depressed without playing it again is a technique that allows pianists to get out of tight fingering spots while still connecting notes that need a legato touch.

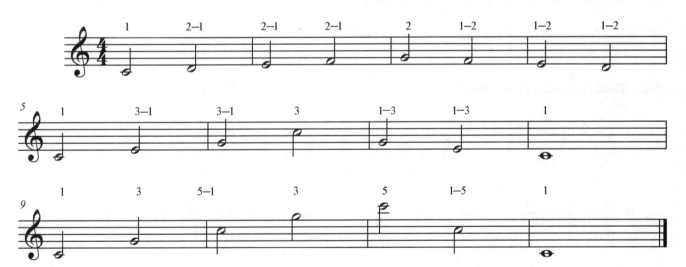

## Baroque Finger-Over-Finger Exercises

It's important to remember that the big powerful instrument we play today is not the same instrument that Beethoven, or even Chopin and Brahms, wrote for, and it has even less in common with the keyboards of the Baroque era. Indeed, much of the keyboard music written before about 1780 wasn't even written for the piano; it was written for organ or harpsichord. Even the music that was written for piano was written for the much frailer pianoforte, which is a very different instrument than today's piano. Sustain pedals are nonexistent on harpsichords and organs, so on those instruments, all legato has to be done with fingers alone.

You've already been introduced to some of the challenges of playing legato. Remember Chapter 14, in which you learned to connect some notes when moving from chord to chord? The same technique can be applied to passage work as well.

 **Track 55a, Example 1**

Similarly, sometimes two fingers have to move over each other at the same time, as in the following exercise.

 **Track 55b (0:20), Example 2**

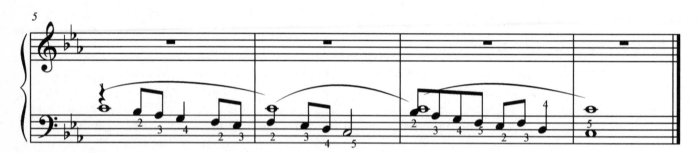

## Competing Hands

Sometimes the hands play so closely together that they are actually playing over each other, with the fingers intertwined. The following exercise copies a rhythmic riff found in Debussy's "le Petit Noir." In this exercise, try playing the right hand sitting on top of the left hand, and then the left hand sitting on top of the right hand. Pianists are about evenly divided about how this should be played. In favor of the left over the right is the fact that it is the left hand doing the moving. But if you play the right hand on top, you can see what both hands are doing.

**Track 56, Example 3**

# Alternate Fingerings

Sometimes, musicians come up with fingerings that seem downright weird. Sometimes the reasons are practical: composers may suggest unusual fingerings or hand distributions to bring out a certain kind of feeling or effect, or to get the performer to think about the music a certain way, or to aid students with small hands.

Bedrich Smetana's *Czech Dance #8*, called "Obkrocak," has an interesting fingering, suggested by the composer himself: one finger is supposed to play the melody of the right hand to force a crisp and bright staccato. You can use this section of music as a staccato exercise. To hear the difference in sound, try to play it both ways—with the one-finger staccato, as written by the composer, and with a traditional fingering (which will be immediately obvious). Chances are, the traditional fingering will be much easier, but the staccatos may not be as crisp.

For an example of how refingering can help a small hand, take Beethoven's "Moonlight Sonata." On the first page, there's a ninth that many pianists with smaller hands have trouble reaching. Look at the passage as originally written, below—and then at the simple and elegant solution of playing that troublesome note with the left hand (note that the sustain pedal must be used in conjunction with this solution).

If you have small hands, you can often omit notes. Notes that are repeated, such as octaves and fifths, put a chord tone into the chord, but in a different hand.

Other unusual fingerings come to us through historical styles. And knowing these techniques can give a pianist more options when fingering a tricky run with black notes in all the wrong places, or help to achieve a legato sound. Good fingering is therefore a key technique for ergonomic and artistic playing.

## The Least You Need to Know

- Effective fingering choices require thinking not only about how to get to a note, but also how to get to the next note, and the one after that.
- Substituting fingers on a note while it is held and passing fingers over each other can create a legato effect, even when it seems a legato effect is impossible.
- Hand-over-hand playing is not just a matter of showing off; sometimes it's the most efficient way to play a passage.
- Composers and editors sometimes suggest difficult and unusual fingerings for artistic reasons.

# Variations on a Theme by Hanon

### In This Chapter

- Introduction to the traditional Hanon technique exercises
- Adapting the Hanon exercises to gain fluency in multiple keys
- Adapting the Hanon exercises to work with chords in all keys
- Adapting the Hanon exercises to develop hand independence
- Adapting the Hanon exercises to work with rhythmic variation

Almost every piano student at the intermediate or advanced level will recognize the name "Hanon." Frenchman Charles-Louis Hanon was a nineteenth-century piano teacher and pedagogue, and in case you haven't yet made his acquaintance, he developed a series of exercises that he claimed would develop equal strength among the five unequal fingers, and lead to virtuosity.

Since then, millions of piano students have struggled with Hanon's finger gymnastics. They are part of the traditional pianist's core curriculum of technical exercises.

This chapter uses these iconic exercises as a jumping-off point, and offers dozens of ways to adapt them to develop fluency in playing in all keys. This chapter also includes variations to help with developing hand independence, adding chords to the mix, and practicing altered rhythms. As it turns out, the creative pianist can find dozens of ways to use Hanon's exercises in ways that Hanon apparently never envisioned.

## Hanon Basics

All of the Hanon exercises use the same basic template. They start on a "home note," which is the first note of a simple eight-note pattern.

In the next measure, the pianist plays the same pattern starting on the next note of the scale.

This continues for two octaves, and then the pattern reverses and goes downhill. This first exercise is the easiest, so students should return to it whenever trying a new variation.

 **Track 57, Example 1**

This first exercise sets the stage for all the rest, which use different combinations of fingers and notes, but follow the same template of an eight-note pattern that is repeated on subsequent notes of the scale:

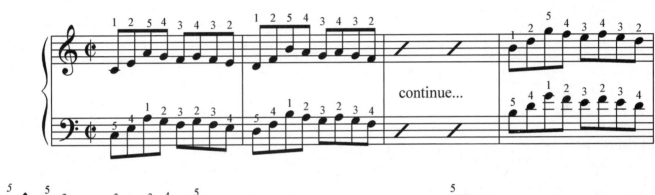

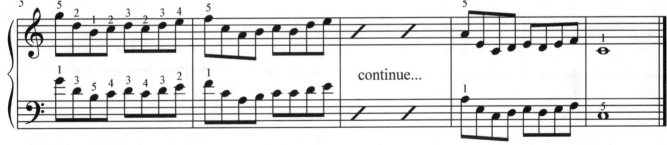

 **THEORY AND PRACTICE**

Today's music stores, not to mention the Internet, are filled with methods that promise a quicker, gentler way to learn piano.

A hundred years ago, it was no different. In fact, Charles-Louis Hanon developed his method as a sort of quick fix to the problem that piano repertoire had gotten too difficult for casual players to handle. "Mediocrity on the instrument is no longer acceptable," he wrote. "It is our goal to combine in one book special exercises which make possible a complete study of piano in far less time." "Far less time" must be a relative phrase, however, because Hanon prescribed playing his entire volume of 60 exercises every day as a solution to technical difficulties.

# Other Hanon Patterns

Most intermediate and advanced pianists already have a volume of Hanon exercises in their libraries, or are destined to get one eventually. If you have a Hanon book, use it as the basis for the adapted exercises described in this chapter.

If you don't, the following Hanon patterns can be used in any of the exercises described in this chapter.

**Pattern 1**

**Pattern 3**

**Pattern 4**

*continues*

*continued*

**Pattern 5**

**Pattern 6**

To learn each new pattern, start in the original key of C and practice the eight-note pattern one hand at a time. When you've learned the pattern, pick up your hand, set it down on the same note in a different octave, and play the pattern again. Then try setting your hand down anywhere on the keyboard, on different starting notes, and playing the pattern. When you can play it anywhere on the keyboard, you are ready to play the entire exercise. Start with one hand at a time so that your fingers don't "get confused."

# Tips for Practicing the Hanon Exercises

In this chapter, we look at some of the many ways to use and adapt Hanon's exercises: changing keys, adding chords, altering rhythms, and playing with dynamics and articulation. Whether learning the original exercises in the original key of C Major, or syncopating the exercises in different keys with chord accompaniments, the pianist should apply the following practice techniques:

- Hand shape should be rounded, with the fingers pressing the keys with the pads near the fingertips, but not with the nails themselves.

- When transposing Hanon exercises, the fingers should play the white keys in the middle third of the key, as close to the black keys as possible. This makes it possible to play quickly on both white and black keys, without having to move the hand excessively back and forth.

- When the thumb or fifth finger is required to play a black note, move the wrist slightly up and forward; this slides the shorter outer fingers in closer to the black notes.

- Play the exercises with a metronome. Most pianists tend to speed up or slow down. Start at about 60 beats per minute, with each beat getting four sixteenth notes (four notes of the eight-note pattern). The advanced pianist should be able to play cleanly at about 108 beats per minute. But accuracy, evenness of tone, and being able to synchronize the hands so that they play precisely at the same time are more important than speed.

- At fast tempos, emphasize the first note of each group of sixteenth notes, at least at first. This will help keep the fingers of each hand synchronized, and avoid one hand running away from the timing of the other hand.

- Keep the wrist firm but relaxed. Most of the work should come from the fingers, with high finger action, but the wrist should not be clenched tight.

- Aim for an even and precise legato, played mezzo-forte. Later in the chapter, we discuss using other touches and volumes.

- Follow the fingerings given. Some of them are counterintuitive, but they help develop your ability to operate your hands independently of one another.

As always, when performing exercises that focus on strength and speed, don't overdo it. At first, five or ten minutes of this kind of intense technical work is more than enough.

**SOUR NOTES**

Be careful not to overdo it. Hanon exercises can be tiring for pianists who are new to them, and too much of the same activity can lead to repetitive stress injuries such as carpal tunnel syndrome. Fortunately, the exercises in this chapter encourage the use of different hands doing different things, different hand positions, different touches, and even different chords. If you start feeling strained, either take a break or switch the exercises—you have plenty to choose from.

# Multi-Key Hanon Exercises

Transposing the Hanon exercises is one of the best ways you can become familiar with and fluent in all keys. The original version is written only on white notes. But playing these exercises in all the keys can turn them into a resource that will help you to become technically proficient in all keys.

To start, let's return to the first Hanon exercise. Remember that this is the simple ascending and descending pattern:

To transpose this to the key of G, simply start on G, skip a note, go up until you run out of fingers, and then go back down. The thumb lands on A, and you start the pattern again—only this time, instead of playing the F (the last note of the pattern), play an F♯ because the key of G has an F♯ in it.

Once you have mastered the first exercise in the key of G, it's time to do other exercises in the same key. (Some of the patterns are written out in this chapter.)

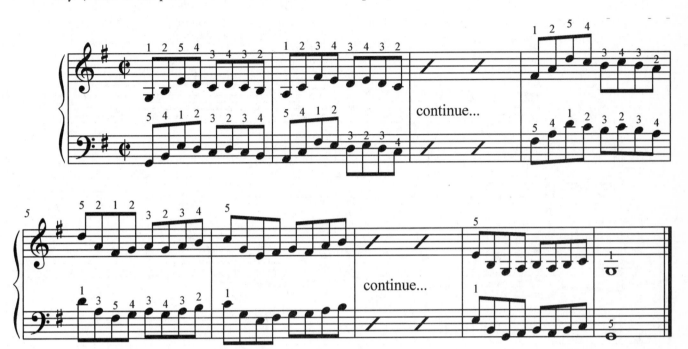

Once you've mastered the key of G, start going through the Circle of Fifths, playing in D, A, E, and B. Then start with the flat keys, playing F, B♭, E♭, A♭, D♭, and G♭.

Always start with the easy Exercise 1 to get your bearings and to give your fingers a chance to understand and feel the geography of the new key.

## Adding Chords

Another way to use the transposed Hanon exercises is to bring chords into the mix. If you want to play rock, jazz, and pop music, you need an almost instinctive familiarity with which chords are which, in all inversions and combinations up and down the piano. If you want to improvise, play songs using a lead sheet, or play by ear. You should be able to throw a hand down on the piano and pick out the notes of any chord without even thinking about it.

Chapter 7 gave some chord drills and improvisation exercises for learning and becoming fluent in the diatonic chords in every key. By playing the transposed Hanon exercises in one hand, and the related chords in the other hand, you can up the ante by playing the chords and the patterns together quickly and in time. This exercise increases both chord fluency and fluency in the different diatonic patterns.

## Chord Exercises for Intermediate Players

Starting in the key of C makes the chord exercises easy to understand. In the key of C, all of the chords use only white notes, so they are easy to find. Once you have graduated to the intermediate level, you should use triads: the three-note chord that starts on the same note the right hand is starting on.

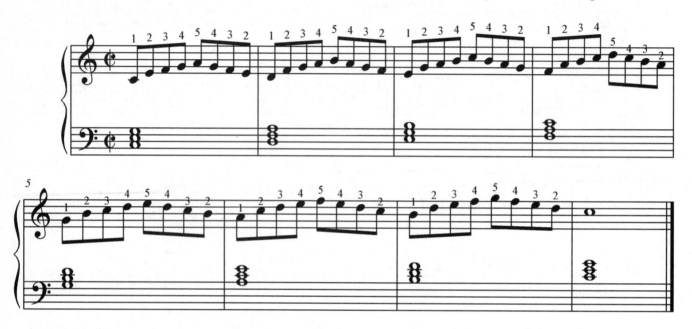

Be sure to switch between hands so that each hand has a chance to learn the chords, and each hand gets a chance to play the Hanon patterns.

Now look at how this changes when you move to the key of G. The key of G has an F♯, so you need to remember to not play an F♮—not only in the Hanon patterns, but also in any of the chords.

In more complex keys, there's a bit more work to handle the patterns in one hand and the chords in the other. Take A♭ for example:

If you find yourself becoming confused as you work your way through the keys, try writing out the names of the chords in each key. Over time, the goal is to be able to play the exercises without any visual cues other than the basic pattern in the original key.

## Advanced Players

If you are an advanced player, you may add diatonic sevenths to all of the chords. This is a bit tricky, so start in the key of C to become familiar with the sound of each chord. Remember that the goal is to be able to play the chords and the patterns with both the right and left hands. The following example has the left hand playing the exercise and the right hand playing the chords. In the key of C, this would give the following pattern:

In A♭, the exercise would look like this:

An advanced variation, for those who are up to a real challenge, is to play the chords in different inversions. Another difficult variation is to play the chords in different voicings. For example, instead of playing all four notes of a seventh chord, only play the first, the third, and the seventh. The purpose of these exercises is not only to develop finger dexterity, but also the mental dexterity necessary to be fluent in all keys. At first, choose easier keys and exercises, play slowly, and feel free to write down the names of the chords.

# Hanon and Hand Independence

In Chapter 15, you learned how to play staccato in one hand and legato in the other. You also practiced playing piano in one hand and forte in the other. The Hanon exercises can be used to develop your skills in both techniques.

Intermediate players should start in the key of C. Remember to start slowly and deliberately until the action of playing one way in one hand and another way in the other hand feels automatic. Be sure to switch which hand is doing what; many students find that it's easy to play one way (for example, left-hand staccato, right-hand legato), but not the other (for example, left-hand legato, right-hand staccato).

 **Track 58, Example 2**

Advanced players who have worked through some of the transposition exercises should be able to handle the hand independence exercises in any key.

# Rhythmic Variation

Hanon exercises can also be used to develop rhythmic fluency. The traditional way to play these exercises is with a metronome. Change the rhythm patterns to emphasize different fingers in the pattern, using the rhythms in the example below.

 **Track 59, Example 3**

Try applying these rhythmic and accent variations to any of the Hanon exercises, starting, as usual, with the first exercise in the key of C and then moving on to more difficult exercises and more difficult keys. Advanced players, however, should be able to transpose the exercises fairly quickly after mastering the basic rhythmic alterations.

## The Least You Need to Know

- The famous Hanon exercises can be adapted and used in many ways to help a pianist learn different skills.

- Transposing the exercises into all keys, rather than staying on only the white keys, makes these exercises an excellent resource for multi-key technique development.

- When transposing or trying a new technique, start with the first exercise—it's much easier than any of the subsequent ones.

- You can adapt the Hanon exercises for use as exercises for rhythmic variation, hand balance, legato and staccato touch, and even playing with chords.

# Advanced Skills

What's left? Plenty, as it turns out. The exercises in this part introduce you to more technically challenging skills, such as pounding the keyboard with double-octave scales (that means playing octaves in both hands at the same time), or racing up and down the keyboard in a cascade of sparkly arpeggios.

You'll also learn about advanced rhythms, so that you can put five beats in one measure and six in another and not lose your groove. And finally, you'll learn to take on ornaments: those curlicues and filigrees that can give us graceful little decorative notes or pounding tremolos.

# Teaching Your Fingers to Fly

## In This Chapter

- Learning to read ahead to tackle difficult passages
- Playing right-hand and left-hand jumps
- Playing with crossed hands
- Playing without looking

By now, you've learned enough technique that you can probably tackle intermediate classical repertoire, four-part hymns for church, and popular songs from songbooks. And you've also learned that how you practice is at least as important as what you practice.

You're now at a point where, if you want, you can use the skills you already know to happily play thousands of pieces of music in a variety of styles. Then again, perhaps you have a hankering to play a particular piece that strikes you as being difficult, or maybe even impossible. In this chapter, I'll cover techniques for more advanced students that will add a few more tools to your toolbox.

## Looking Ahead

As music becomes more difficult and more complex, it likely has more notes, faster tempi, bigger jumps, and more complex rhythm combinations.

This is where good reading skills become extremely important. A good music reader identifies notes quickly, but she also looks at the intervals between them. She can look at a rhythm figure containing dotted notes and notes of different values, and know instantly how the pattern goes. She recognizes chords and scale fragments, and can identify basic underlying harmonic patterns—but most of all, this musician looks ahead.

Why look ahead? Consider what you do when driving a car. A good driver doesn't only look at what's right in front of her. While driving, her eyes dart this way and that, and she tries to be sure to remember what's behind her, notices what's coming up on either side, and takes note of the kid wobbling dangerously on a bike on the side of the road. At the same time, the driver also looks ahead to see what's coming up: a railroad crossing, a truck pulling out, or a red light. A good driver doesn't wait until she is halfway through the intersection before noticing the red light; because she has already looked ahead, she was ready to stop.

It's exactly the same for a pianist playing a piece of music, especially when what's coming up requires big leaps across the piano, a big change of hand position, or a key change. It's much easier to move your hands two octaves in either direction when you know you're going to have to do it before you actually have to do it. But if you are reading music one note at a time, looking only at the note you are playing, you have no warning. You are always playing catch-up.

**THEORY AND PRACTICE**

The best way to up your reading-ahead skills is to sight read. Choose music that is well below your current playing level. Start with slow, easy pieces. The goal is to play everything in time, even if that means missing a few notes here and there. If you're an intermediate player, you might even choose books that are in the performance component of a graded method book. It's best if you don't already know how the piece goes so you don't "cheat" by letting your ears help you.

## Seeing Melodic Patterns

Recognizing patterns helps with reading because our brains make connections between similar things. So if a piece of music has a repeating motif or phrase, our brain will compare those motifs and phrases to what it already knows. The following exercise is a reading drill. Before beginning to play it, tell yourself what happens in the music. Can you identify the chord pattern? Can you tell which scales and modes you have to play? What about repeated material? Notes in the piece should help you. Tell yourself the story of the piece—then, and only then, try to play it.

## Seeing Harmonic Patterns

Similarly, recognizing harmonic patterns can be a big help when navigating a thicket of prickly chords. Remember, in many popular songs, the harmonies often use just three or four chords. Even if they use a few others, those are the exceptions rather than the rule. In the following example, the chords repeat over and over: if you can identify them, you shouldn't even have to think about what you are playing with your left hand.

**Track 60, Example 1**

Did you recognize the chord progression when you played it? It's a simplification of a 300-year-old piece of music that is as fresh as yesterday: Pachelbel's "Canon in D," which uses the I, vi, IV, and V chords—just like a thousand popular songs from the last 50 years. By learning these popular chord progressions, and then being able to recognize them, you can vanquish a great deal of the difficulty of reading and learning a new piece.

# Jumps

The piano repertoire has plenty of opportunities for both the right hand and the left hand to jump all over the keyboard. Pianists often use the left hand for this technique in accompaniments, where there is a low bass note followed by an accompaniment pattern in the middle register. Chopin, in particular, favored writing left-hand parts this way, especially for his waltzes and mazurkas.

There are numerous ways to approach this challenge, depending on what else is going on in the piece. For example, if the right hand has a fast scale run, as often happens in Chopin's music, it might be advisable to memorize the right-hand part before trying to play both hands together. That way, you can concentrate on the left-hand notes.

As with the preceding example, knowing what chord you are going to helps you get there faster and more securely. In the following exercise, you use your left hand to play a simple I–IV–V–I cadence, such as you learned in Chapter 7. The patterns are written out for the keys of C, G, and D. Once you've learned the pattern in those keys, go ahead and transpose it into all 12 keys. The only difference between the basic cadence and this exercise is that this time, you are playing them in a 3/4 time pattern with a bass note that requires a giant leap.

**Track 61, Example 2**

Force yourself to practice the left hand without looking. This will give you a more tactile sense of where the notes are and how they fit into the hand. You'll also develop a better sense of your peripheral vision.

Of course, it's perfectly acceptable to quickly glance down at your fingers when necessary, but if you've taken all the other steps outlined about, you may be surprised to find out that you don't need to look down at your hands nearly as much as you think you do.

**FLYING FINGERS**

Keep your hand loosely open when doing big jumps. The beginning and ending points are your top and bottom fingers (usually the thumb and fifth finger), so those are the notes you should be reaching for. The other fingers should practice contracting and expanding to catch the rest of the notes of the chord.

## Two-Handed Jumps

Jumping two hands at a time is even trickier, especially if they are moving in different directions or in different intervals.

Try the following octave jumps. You should be thinking ahead to the next note when you start playing the note before it. You may need to practice each jump separately. You may also want to practice each hand separately before trying to play both hands together.

The next exercise is a little more difficult, involving jumps in both hands and some eight-note octave passages. If you haven't played octave scales yet, check out Chapter 20, which has more on this important technique. For now, play the passage slowly.

 **Track 62, Example 3**

# Cross-Hand Playing

It seems like it should be obvious: the right hand plays the high notes on the right-hand side of the piano—let's call it right-hand territory. The left hand behaves itself down in the bass register, in left-hand territory.

Indeed, that's what happens most of the time. But sometimes, composers write passages that are easier to play with the right hand crossing over the left hand or the left hand over the right hand.

But why cross hands other than to show off?

In Chapter 7, you learned to play cross-hand arpeggios by passing one hand over the other and then back again. Cross-hand playing is also required when one hand has an ongoing pattern in the middle of the keyboard, and the music calls for a bass voice to alternate with a treble voice. Believe it or not, it's actually easier to cross the hands over each other than to interrupt the flow of the middle voice and move both hands to a new position.

Sometimes the crossover is for just one note, when one hand has finished a passage, and the other hand can easily reach over and hit a final high note or low note. Sometimes the hands take turns crossing over each other to move up and down the keyboard, as in a cross-hand arpeggio. And sometimes, the hands cross back and forth to play entire lines of music.

In some pieces, one hand stays in one place, playing a repeated accompaniment pattern in the middle of the keyboard, while the other hand plays a call-and-response type of melody, first in the left hand, then answering in the right hand. It's much easier to play these kinds of pieces with crossed hands than to try to move both hands while maintaining continuity in the middle part. Even if it were possible, most pianists would choose to play with crossed hands because of energy flow, and because they can better control the dynamics of the various parts by having the right hand play the call and response, and the left hand play a continuous accompaniment. Plus, as one of my teenaged students says, "it looks really, really impressive."

**Track 63, Example 4**

# Look Mom, No Eyes!

Earlier in this chapter, I talked about the value of looking ahead when reading music. Now consider not looking at all when practicing. And by that, I mean practicing difficult passages with your eyes closed.

I'm not speaking here of memorizing an entire piece for performance. I'm talking about practicing small snippets of technically challenging phrases until you can play them with your eyes closed.

You probably don't think you can do it. But pick a piece of music you know really well, and choose a section of it that was tough to learn. See what happens if you close your eyes and try to play some of the parts you had to practice most often to learn. I bet you make some mistakes. But I also bet you do better than you thought you would.

**THEORY AND PRACTICE**

The young Japanese pianist Nobuyuki Tsujii shared first prize in the 2009 International Van Cliburn Competition. What is unusual is not only that first prize was awarded to two contestants—but also that Tsujii is blind. Nonetheless, he attacked the great romantic warhorses such as the Rachmaninoff's knuckle-bending "Second Piano Concerto" as though it was absurd to think anyone should have to look when moving hands all over the keyboard.

Being able to play a difficult passage with your eyes closed will give you an enormous sense of security when you have to perform. For ensemble players, knowing difficult sections so well you can play them blindfolded means you can concentrate more on looking at your colleagues and less on looking at your fingers.

## The Least You Need to Know

- Reading ahead and identifying harmonic and melodic patterns can help pianists tackle tricky passages.
- Use your peripheral vision to tackle big leaps.
- Playing with crossed hands allows for the pianist to achieve continuity in the middle voice; it's not just about showing off.
- Practicing with your eyes closed can give you added security and a greater sense of the feel and sound of the music.

# Full Arpeggios

**Chapter**

# 19

## In This Chapter

- Practicing arpeggios to achieve a smooth sound
- Mastering the thumb-under, fingers-over fingering
- Playing triad arpeggios in major and minor keys
- Learning the different kinds of four-note arpeggios

In Chapter 7, you learned some basic one-octave arpeggios. You also learned to move up and down the keyboard using a simple cross-hand chord pattern. But arpeggios can be played in many ways, with simple triad chords, or with more complex chords such as sixth and seventh chords. Arpeggios can shimmer all over the piano, and are used in music from the Classical period through popular contemporary music (and perhaps overused in so-called cocktail music). For classical musicians, they are an essential tool. For improvisers, they are a reliable accompaniment pattern.

## Technical Challenges

The basic technical issue in playing arpeggios is achieving an even, pearl-like tone while passing the thumb under the fingers or the fingers over the thumb. This is, of course, the same technical issue we face in playing scales, except that in the arpeggio, the thumb must pass under the fingers and then stretch two or sometimes three notes away.

Here is a basic C Major arpeggio for the right hand. Going up, the thumb of the right hand passes under the fingers after the third finger plays G. Coming down, the third finger of the right hand passes over the thumb after the thumb plays the second C. If you are like most pianists just starting to play multi-octave arpeggios, you probably play it in triplets, with the thumb getting a slight accent, and maybe even with a slight break between each G and each C.

**Track 64a, Example 1**

This is exactly how you *don't* want it to sound! Instead, try to play it in 3/4 time, with each beat divided into sixteenth notes. Notice that the beat is clearly stressed every fourth note. This helps your hand learn to play the arpeggios evenly, no matter where the finger turns and position changes fall.

**Track 64b (0:10), Example 2**

It can be tricky to play finger turns with a smooth legato and controlled even dynamics. Letting the arms move freely during the turns helps carry the fingers toward the note. The wrists should move slightly upward to allow the thumb to more easily pass under the fingers. It also helps to allow the wrists to move freely in a circular motion.

# Fingering Arpeggios

The fingerings of the white-note arpeggios are based on the fingerings you learned in Chapter 7, with the addition of the thumb pass, which is necessary to play a second, third, or fourth octave.

The fingerings for arpeggios that start on black notes are completely different than the fingerings you played in Chapter 7. Don't be intimidated by black-note arpeggios The thumb pass under a finger that is on a black note is much easier to perform smoothly than it is when playing most white-note arpeggios. The exceptions are the keys of G♭ and E♭ minor, both of which contain only black notes. The arpeggios in these two keys are the most difficult to play because the thumb lands insecurely on a black note.

In the following examples, the suggested fingerings follow patterns. For example, almost all the major arpeggios starting on white notes use the same fingering. You need to learn to internalize the correct fingerings automatically, so complete fingerings are written out for the first arpeggio in each category. Beyond that, I've indicated where there are anomalies, or when there might be some confusion.

The following examples are written for arpeggios played over two octaves. To extend the arpeggios to three or four octaves, however, requires simply repeating the same pattern and fingerings in the next octave. As soon as you are able, practice four-octave arpeggios to develop fluency all over the keyboard. Three-octave arpeggios are not recommended for practicing arpeggios of three-note chords because the rhythm doesn't work out evenly.

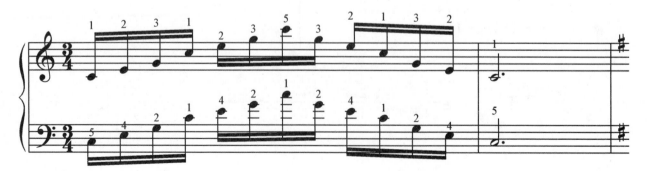

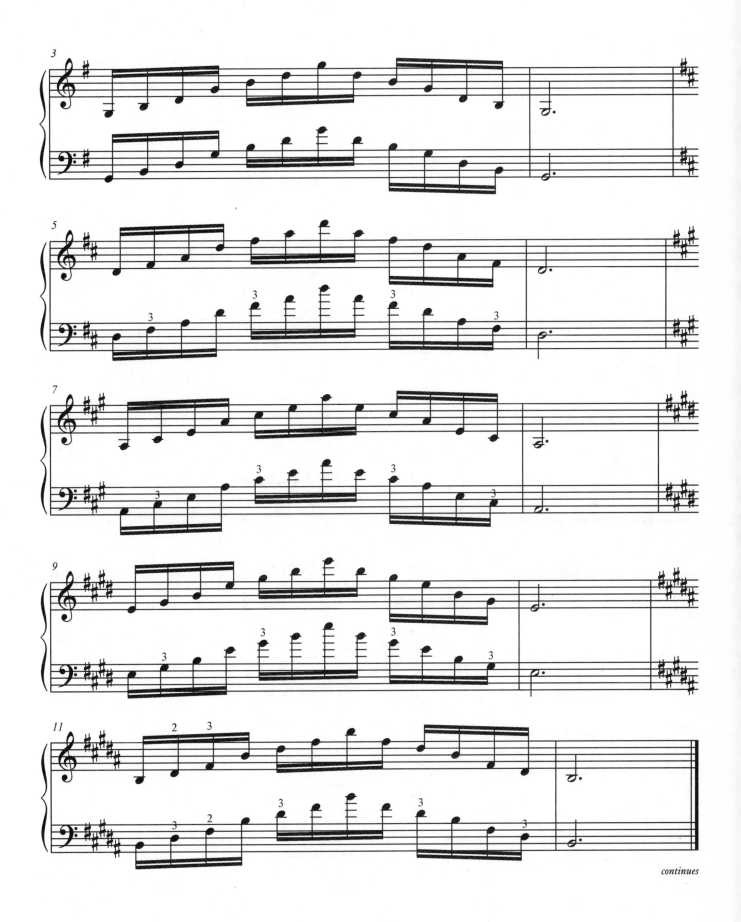

*continues*

*continued*

*continues*

*continued*

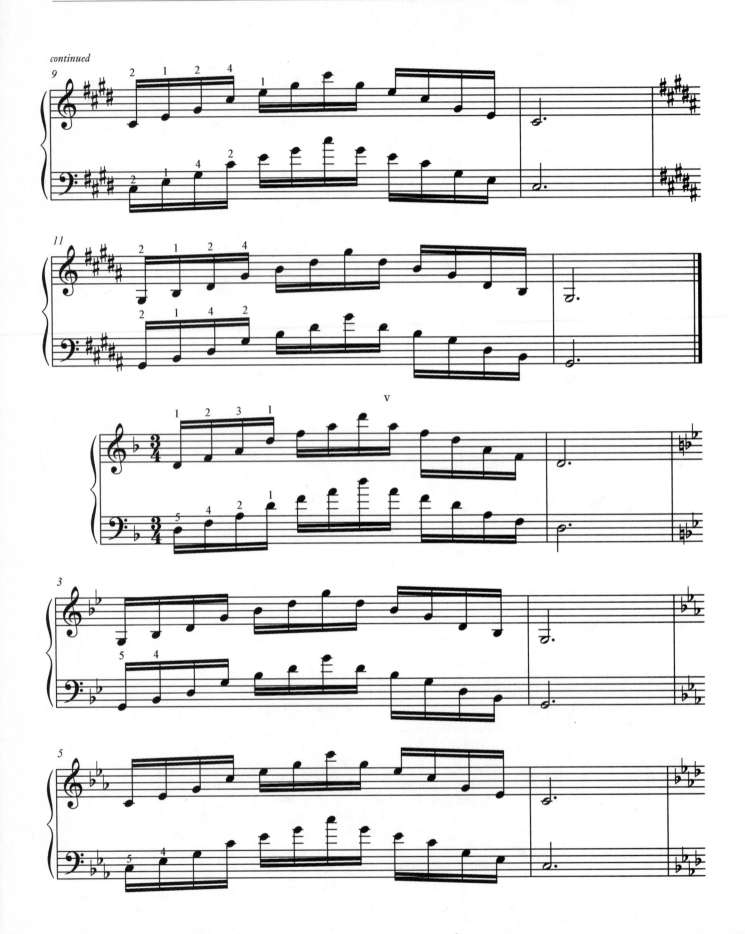

## Practice Exercises for Smoother Arpeggios

As with anything, it pays to isolate the trouble spots in an arpeggio and practice playing them alone. Take the key of B Major, which requires a larger than normal stretch on the thumb pass in the right hand.

For the right hand, the trouble area is moving from the F♯ to the B, and then repositioning the hand to hit the D♯.

These three notes need to be practiced. You don't have to memorize the following exercise, or even play it note for note—you can improvise your own. The key is to isolate and repeat the trouble spot. In the recorded examples, you'll first hear the right-hand exercise as written, and then you'll hear an example of continuing to work on this technique. Notice that the example is played in strict time. The exercise is then repeated for the left hand, which has a different trouble spot, because the fingers pass over each other on different notes.

**Track 65a, Example 3**

improvise right hand exercise....

**Track 65b (0:26), Example 4**

continue improvising

Like almost anything on the piano, arpeggios take time to master. Practice one hand at a time, playing the thumb-under/fingers-over part separately. Don't try to put hands together until your fingerings are secure and you are comfortable with the thumb pass. Practice two-octave and four-octave arpeggios, and be sure to play in strict metric time. Three-note chords should be played with four notes to the beat.

**FLYING FINGERS**

Just as with scales, arpeggios are used in music very differently than they are practiced. Composers may skip notes (particularly in the bass, where it is common to spread out the beginning notes of arpeggios), and they often use arpeggios in inversions. Fingerings for these can vary widely, depending on the key, as well as what has come before and what comes after the arpeggio. It's not uncommon for the composer to throw in an extra note or two, which also affects fingerings. Mastering the basic root position fingerings, however, will prepare you to deal with these variations when they occur.

# At Sixes and Sevens

So far we've looked at only three-note arpeggios based on our basic triads. Four-note arpeggios are also common, especially the four-note fully diminished seventh chord, the sixth chord, and various other types of seventh chords, most commonly the dominant seventh. With four-note chords, use a triplet rhythm and accentuate every third note to avoid always coming down hard on the thumb. Four-note chords should be practiced over a span of three octaves, because it parses with the three-note rhythmic groupings.

The following exercise includes these four-note arpeggios: the sixth chord, the dominant seventh, and the major seventh, starting on C. You can do this exercise starting on any note of the keyboard.

Diminished chords are four-note chords in which each note is spaced a step and a half (a minor third) away from every other note. The diminished chords that start on C, E♭, G♭, and A actually contain the same notes; they just start in a different position, as shown next. There are three sets of diminished chords:

- The set containing the notes C, E♭, G♭, and A

- The set containing D♭, E, G, and B♭

- The set containing D, F, A♭, and B

Because of enharmonic notes (for example, an A♭ is the same as a G♯), there may be different spellings for some arpeggios. Music theory dictates which spellings are correct. The following example uses the simplest possible correct spellings.

**THEORY AND PRACTICE**

What, you might reasonably ask, is a "double flat"? Music theory tells us that a seventh chord contains a triad, plus a "seventh." We've already learned that a major seventh chord uses the seventh from the major scale (in the key of C, that's a B). The dominant seventh chord uses the flatted seventh (a half step down from the major seventh; in the key of C, that's a B♭). And—get ready for this—a diminished seventh is a half step down from the dominant seventh. But because all the sevenths in the key of C have to be called "B," we sometimes call the diminished seventh a "B double flat." Simple answer: When you see a double flat, just go down a whole step. A B double flat is the same note as an A, even if you can't (technically speaking) call it that.

## The Least You Need to Know

- Arpeggios are used as accompaniment patterns in all styles of music.
- Playing arpeggios requires practicing the fingerings, especially the turns in which the thumb passes under the fingers, and vice versa.
- Three-note arpeggios include the major and minor triads.
- Four-note arpeggios include sixth, dominant seventh, major seventh, and diminished seventh chords.

# Scale Olympics: Swifter, Higher, Stronger

### In This Chapter

- Playing scales in thirds, sixths, and tenths
- Playing scales in broken octaves
- Learning the broken octave blues bass
- Playing scales in octaves

In Chapters 8 through 12, you spent a great deal of time learning all the scales: majors and minors, as well as the minor variations, the modes, and a few other scales.

You've learned that, unlike scales in practice, scales in actual music often involve variations on textbook techniques. In this chapter, I'll show you some more advanced scale techniques and practice exercises that will prepare you to tackle scales in trickier technical passages.

## Thirds, Sixths, and Tenths

Scales often appear in music with one hand starting on one note, while the other hand starts on another note, usually at an interval of a third, a sixth, or a tenth. A tenth is simply a third plus an octave (and you're right if you think this doesn't make mathematical sense). If you've learned all the modes, as discussed in Chapter 10, you understand that when scales are played in intervals such as thirds and sixths, one hand is playing the parent scale while the other is playing a mode of that scale.

For example, look at the C scale, played with the left hand following along a sixth below the right hand.

Notice that the common left-hand fingering (5–4–3–2–1–3–2–1) works for the left hand playing the C scale starting on E (the Phrygian mode, if you recall). The fingering you choose to use in any piece of music depends on the key you are playing in, as well as where the scale starts and ends, the speed, whether any other notes are introduced, and other factors. There's no way to practice all the possible fingerings and variations, but if you make a habit of practicing scales in different keys and combinations, you'll be well-prepared to adjust to whatever music you put in front of you.

In the next example, it's the right hand that plays the Phrygian mode a third above the left hand, which plays the parent scale of C Major.

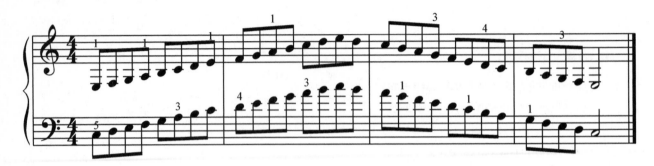

In the next exercise, the left hand follows a third below the right hand. If you've mastered your minor scales, you'll see that the left hand is simply playing the A minor scale while the right hand plays the C Major scale.

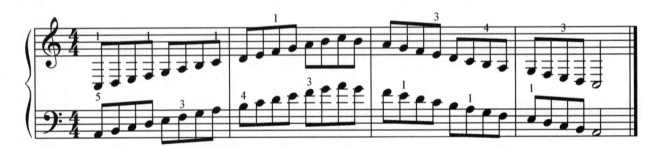

The scale in tenths is simply a scale played in thirds, with an added octave, but it has a very different sound.

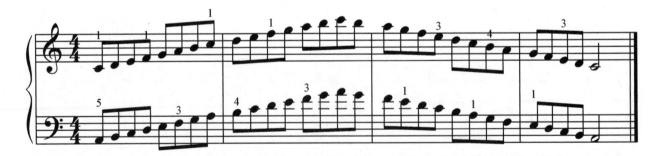

Now go back and apply these techniques to other scales you learned in Chapters 8 through 12. These are best practiced over a span of at least two octaves, but if a two-octave run is too confusing, start by playing just one octave.

Finally, take a look at how this kind of pattern might show up in a more musical context.

**Track 66, Example 1**

# Broken Octaves

Broken octaves are patterns played with one or both hands alternating notes between octaves, as shown in this example:

**Track 67a, Example 2**

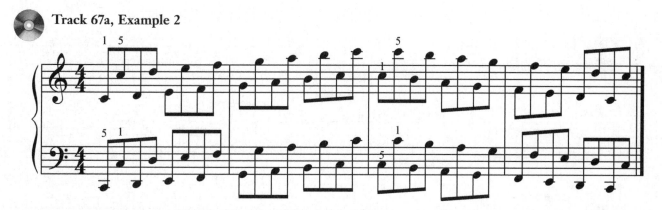

Broken octaves are an important technique because they help teach the hand to feel the distance of an octave. As you practice these, try to feel how far your fingers need to move each time you shift position to play a new octave. Try these exercises with your eyes closed as well. The ability to quickly and accurately feel an octave is a technique that advanced players use, no matter what style of music they are playing.

All scales can be practiced in broken octaves, first with hands separate, then with hands together. If your hand is big enough, try playing broken octaves with your fourth finger playing black notes and your fifth finger playing white notes. Your hand may not be big enough to make this reach, especially in the descending scale, in which you have to stretch a ninth. But if you can reach, it's a more secure fingering.

Broken octaves also appear in chromatic scales, often with both hands playing together. To practice, start with one hand at a time, and then try putting them together. As with the diatonic scales, try to use your fourth finger on the black notes (if you can reach).

**Track 67b (0:09), Example 3**

Here's one more reason to learn to play broken octaves: remove just two notes from the scale, flat the seventh, and you have a typical blues bass.

# Octaves and Double Octaves

Scales also can be played in octaves, either in one hand or in both hands at the same time (often referred to as "double octaves"). These should be practiced with each hand alone and then hands together.

For very fast octave scales, try fixing the distance between your fingers and holding your hand fairly static in that position, but allow the wrist to bounce (sort of like bouncing a basketball). This takes a bit of practice, because it's hard to hold the fingers in a fairly fixed position while keeping the wrist flexible.

**SOUR NOTES**

Don't overdo it on the virtuoso octaves! These exercises put a lot of strain on your wrists. Like any athletic endeavor, your muscles need to build up to the point where they can take on strenuous tasks. Practice a minute or two each day, and build up slowly, to avoid carpal tunnel syndrome.

To practice controlling the movement of your octaves, start by playing the first octave, and then bouncing on that note four times. Then move to the next note, and bounce on that note four times. Try to put the accent on the first set of notes and then allow your wrist to bounce for the other three. Do this all the way up the scale.

 **Track 68a, Example 4**

Once you can do that, try the same bouncing technique. But while you are bouncing, move your wrist so you are playing four different notes.

**Track 68b (0:11), Example 5**

Finally—after doing these exercises for each hand separately—put them together in double octaves.

 **Track 68c (0:29), Example 6**

## The Least You Need to Know

- Scales can be played at intervals, with one hand playing the scale starting on one note and the other hand starting on another note.
- Scales are often played at intervals of thirds, sixths, and tenths.
- Practicing broken octaves is a good way for the hand to learn the important skill of automatically reaching for an octave.
- Scales in octaves and double octaves can be practiced using a bouncing wrist motion.

# Advanced Rhythms

## In This Chapter

- Learning to count and play in unusual time signatures
- Learning to play and count in changing meter
- Learning to play and count polyrhythms
- Learning to play and count syncopation

It's true you could spend your whole life playing music and never run out of interesting, artistic, challenging pieces to play that have two, three, or four beats to a measure. But then you'd miss out on Dave Brubeck's "Take Five," or Tchaikovsky's "Pathetique" Symphony, or Neil Young's "Words," or Mussorgsky's "Pictures at an Exhibition." And that's just the beginning of rhythmic variation!

Complex rhythms include unusual time signatures, varying and sometimes unpredictable combinations of time signatures, and unusual ways of dividing measures into rhythmic sub-units that are not typically even. They also include syncopation as well as compound rhythms, in which one hand is playing in one rhythmic pattern while the other hand plays in a different rhythmic pattern.

## Unusual Time Signatures

Unusual time signatures simply have a different number of beats in a measure than you may be used to. For example, Dave Brubeck's "Take Five" has five beats to a measure. It's also possible to have 7 beats to a measure, or 11, or however many the composer can imagine. But as fancy and complicated as all that may sound, generally, when you play in an unusual time signature, what you are really doing is playing in sub-groups of either two or three beats.

Listen to the following chord progression, which is written in 5/4 time. Notice how the music seems to divide itself into a cluster of three beats followed by a cluster of two beats. You can count along saying "ONE-two-three-FOUR-five, ONE-two-three-FOUR-five." You can also use the recorded example to improvise. (A sample right-hand improvisation over the chord progression is also found on the recording.) When you improvise, use the notes of the C Major scale, and play high on the keyboard so you can distinguish between what you are playing and what the recording is playing. Don't worry if you fall out of sync the first few times; 5/4 time is not a natural rhythm for most people, and it takes some getting used to. It helps to count throughout.

**Track 69, Example 1**

When approaching a piece of music written in an unusual time signature, look for the underlying patterns of sub-groupings. Identifying these patterns will help you keep track of the flow of the music and where you are in it.

For example, 9/8 time is not an uncommon time signature; you will usually hear it in three groups of three triplets, as in the first lines of the next example.

But in the second line of music, the rhythmic subdivisions have been altered. The same notes have a completely different sound and feel.

**Track 70a, Example 2**

Now try the next example. It may help for you to count one-two, one-two, one-two-three; one-two, one-two, one-two-three as you play.

Track 70b (0:20), Example 3

## Meter Changes

Composers can also change the meter during the piece, which might mean switching from 4/4 time to a measure of 2/4 time, or changing from 3/4 to 5/4. These changes can be regular—a measure of 5/4 followed by a measure of 4/4, followed by more measures of alternating 5/4 and 4/4. (In that case, the repeating patterns can resemble the 9/8 exercise above; it's just a different way of approaching the same idea.) In Mussorgsky's "Pictures at an Exhibition," the main theme alternates between 5/4 and 6/4 time, before finally settling into 6/4. The uneven meter portrays the idea of a person meandering through an exhibition, pausing and changing stride whenever something catches his attention.

Track 71, Example 4

Try the following rhythm exercise to get used to playing in shifting time signatures. Notice how the measures of 5/4 time seem to be divided into subgroups of three beats followed by two beats.

**Track 72, Example 5**

# Polyrhythms

Polyrhythms are played just like their name suggests: more than one rhythmic figure at a time.

The easiest and most common example of polyrhythms is two against three, in which one hand plays groups of eighth notes while the other hand plays groups of triplets.

**Track 73a, Example 6**

To learn this, get out your metronome and play the example one hand at a time. Start with several triplets followed by several duplets, then alternate triplets with duplets.

It's tricky to put the hands together. The vertical lines in the first measure show where the left-hand notes come in, in relation to where the right-hand notes are played. You might be able to pick this up by listening to the musical example, or you may need to take a more mathematical approach. To do this, look at the sub-beat numbers (in the middle of the staff, from one to six).

**Track 73b (0:11), Example 7**

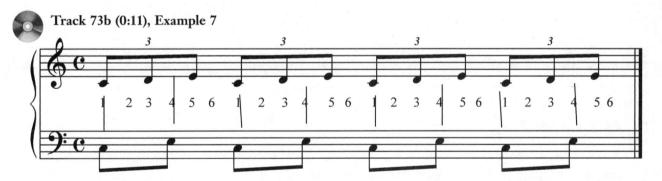

Basically, both hands play on one. You count to two without playing any notes. The right hand plays on three, the left hand plays on four, the right hand plays on five, nothing is played on six, and then it starts all over again with one.

**Track 74, Example 8**

## Three Against Four

An even more complex polyrhythm is three against four. For an example of three against four, look at the following excerpt from Chopin's "Fantasie Impromptu":

**Track 75a, Example 9**

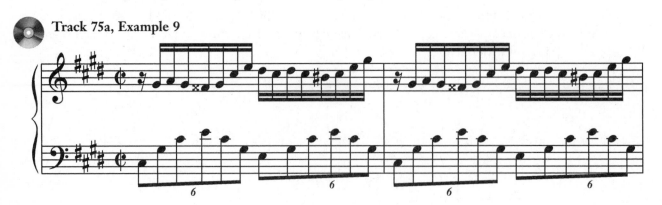

The recorded example is first played at a slow practice tempo, and then at the actual performance tempo. At the slower tempo, you can hear that the right-hand notes and the left-hand notes are not played at the same time. In the two measures recorded here, the right hand plays 32 notes (30 sixteenth notes plus 2 sixteenth note rests), while the left hand plays 24 notes. Here, the example is repeated, and you can see which right-hand notes are supposed to be played with which left-hand notes.

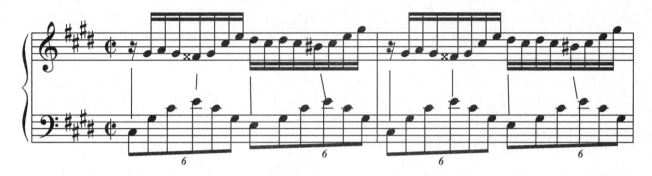

Learning to feel three against four is trickier than playing two against three. As with the three against two example, start by playing the patterns one hand at a time. Here is something a little easier than Chopin to practice.

**Track 75b (0:17), Example 10**

*continues*

In three against four, count to 12. Both hands play on one. The right-hand notes come in on one, four, seven, and ten; the left-hand notes come in on one, five, and nine. Then it starts all over again with one.

# Swing and Syncopation

In standard rhythm, we tend to accentuate the notes that fall on the downbeat, or the strong beat of a measure: usually the first and third beats in 4/4 time, and the first beat in 3/4 time.

With syncopated rhythm, the accent notes come in where we don't expect them. They may come in just before the strong beat, or just after. Syncopation, with its use of anticipation and delay, creates movement and provides a strong rhythmic drive.

In jazz and blues, syncopation is often combined with swing. If a song is to be played in swing, the sheet music usually says so at the beginning, although jazz lead sheets intended for professionals often assume the player knows what to play and what not to play in swing.

**SOUR NOTES**

It's tempting to want to just launch in and start playing a favorite song when you get the lead sheet or sheet music for it. But if it's a jazz or blues tune, stop to work out the counts. Rhythm is the soul of this kind of music, and incorrect rhythms are felt as bumps in the road by your audience. Plus, it's very easy to learn an incorrect rhythm—not so easy to unlearn it. Do yourself a favor and count.

In swing, each beat is divided into two eighth notes, but the eighth notes are played approximately as triplets, with the first eighth note getting a count of "one and" and the second triplet getting a count of "a," as marked in the following exercise. The challenge with syncopation comes in with ties and rests that put the accented note of the music on a weak beat. This creates finger-snapping, toe-tapping rhythms—but it's difficult to learn to count it.

For example, in this exercise, the left hand holds the groove together and the right hand plays against it in grouped swing eighths (which are counted a lot like triplets). It's probably easier to learn it by listening, but the counts are written out next to the notes for the first half of the piece. After that, you'll have to write in your own rhythms. But don't panic! The second half mirrors the first half almost exactly.

**Track 76, Example 11**

It may take a while before counting syncopated rhythms feels at all natural. First of all, it's confusing. Second, syncopated rhythms are often divided into small sub-beats. Playing syncopated music (which includes virtually all jazz and blues) requires the player to have a firm internal metronome—a sense of where the beat falls. The music is played around the underlying structure of the regular beats. Use your metronome to help learn this—it's like having the help of a reliable drummer.

## The Least You Need to Know

- Time signatures can include odd and unusual numbers of beats per measure (within reason), including five and seven.
- Beats in measures can be unevenly divided, usually into groups of twos and threes.
- Counting unusual rhythms is essential to mastering and feeling them.
- In polyrhythms, one hand plays triplets while the other plays in duplet groups of either two or four.
- Syncopation may be easier to feel than to read, but learning to read syncopated time helps with precision and solidifies the groove.

# Ornamentation

## In This Chapter

- Understanding the function of ornaments
- Discovering the types of ornaments and the musical effects they create
- Knowing what notes to play when the music is full of squiggles
- Playing ornaments in a rhythmic context

If you've ever been inside a European church from the Baroque period, you know what ornamentation is: the curlicues on the pillars, the decorative designs, the gold leaf on everything. In music, ornamentation decorates the phrases and draws attention to highlights. It's no surprise that musical ornamentation first flourished during the Baroque period, when all art, it seems, was decorated, curlicued, and ornamented to the last possible inch. In music, performers were expected to add ornaments based on the composer's notation to add to the interpretation.

The symbols for ornaments are a sort of shorthand—little squiggles in different shapes and designs that indicate the series of notes to be played. But the rules are inexact and vary by period. The entire subject of how to precisely realize ornaments could take up an entire book and still leave room for argument. And indeed, musicians frequently disagree with each other about how these little symbols should be performed. In this chapter, I will show you some of the most common ornaments you're likely to encounter, and give you the most commonly accepted ways to play them. The exercises will help you develop the techniques needed to play these fast, elegant figures.

Once you start to encounter ornamentation as a regular part of your musical explorations, it might be worthwhile to run your interpretation by a teacher, who can help you with the fine points of realizing particular figures from particular periods.

## General Rules of Ornamentation

Ornaments generally are notated by putting their symbol immediately above the note to which they pertain (called the principal note). Sometimes, however, an ornament will be between two notes, or just in front of a note.

There is a great deal of debate regarding where ornaments should begin. In other words, should the principal note, the note around which the ornament is constructed, be played first? Or should the upper auxiliary note, the note just above the principal note, be first? For music composed prior to around

1800, the ornamentation begins with the upper auxiliary note. For music written after 1800, however, ornaments often start on the principal note, which creates a more pleasing melodic line. Remember, regardless of the general guidelines, as the performer, you get to decide how you want it played.

**THEORY AND PRACTICE**

In the Baroque period, ornaments were one of the most important tools a performer used to put his own stamp on the music he played. Composers expected performers to ornament the music, sometimes adding so many trills, frills, and doo-thingies that the original tune was all but indiscernible. As a reaction, classical composers started writing in ornaments, and by the Romantic period, performers were expected to follow the specific instructions of the composer much more literally.

If the ornament has no sharps or flats written above or below it, use the notes that are in the scale of the piece. So for example, in the key of G, if the ornament's principal note is E, the upper auxiliary is F♯ (because F♯ is in the key of G); the lower auxiliary is D♮. If a sharp, a flat, or a natural is placed above the ornament, it means that the note above the principal note should be played with a sharp, flat, or natural. The same rule applies to notes below the ornament. So in our example, if a natural sign were placed over the ornament, instead of playing an F♯, you would play an F♮.

# Types of Ornaments

The following ornaments are the most common. Each ornament is shown with its symbol and instructions on how to play it.

## Grace Notes

Grace notes are little introductory notes that are played so quickly that they don't have a rhythmic value. There may be one or two grace notes before a principal note, and all the notes in that group are played squashed (but gracefully) into the same beat. Usually, the grace note starts on the beat and the principal note is played just after the beat, but the effect is that of all the notes existing on the same beat, with the stress on the principal note. Any accidentals for grace notes are placed directly in front of the grace note itself.

The grace note ornament is common throughout classical music, and it's often heard in the blues. In this first example, start by playing the first line as written. Then play the second line, adding the grace notes. The general outline of the melody and rhythm should sound the same, just a little—ornamented.

 **Track 77a, Example 1**

Once you've practiced the melody line, try putting it together with an accompaniment, being sure to stress the principal note after each grace note.

**Track 77b (0:16), Example 2**

In the next example, the grace note is used to add a blue note to the tune. You can hear how the addition of this one quick note changes the feel of the music.

**Track 78, Example 3**

Sometimes the grace note can be played by playing all the notes together and then pulling up the grace note to create a drone effect.

**Track 79, Example 4**

## Trills

Trills are simply a pattern in which the pianist plays the written note alternating with the note just above it. The most common rule is for the trill to start on the upper auxiliary note, meaning that if the note under the trill sign is a C, the trill is played starting on D, then alternating between C and D. This rule, however, is more of a guideline than an absolute edict. It's not uncommon for trills to start on the written note if the melodic passage leads into them.

There are several different ways to finger a trill. Some of them seem initially awkward, but lead to more control and less strain, especially in passages with long trills. Many piano students simply let their strong fingers (usually the second and third) take the lead. But using the first and third fingers is often a better choice, especially when the higher note is a black note. It also may be necessary to trill with the weaker third and fourth fingers, or even the fourth and fifth fingers, if the thumb or other fingers have to hold down a lower note. So practice trills using all combination of fingers.

Note that although the trills are written out in the example, the notes in a trill really don't have an assigned rhythm. The performer decides how many times to go up and down, and how fast to trill. This decision is based on the speed of the music, the duration given to the trill, the character of the music, and what is going on in the other hand.

Trills often end with a turn, which may or may not be notated in the music. For example:

Try this exercise in which the trill in the right hand is played against an Alberti bass in the left hand. Notice that all the trills start on the upper auxiliary in this exercise, except the last one that starts on the principal note to create a more fluid melodic line with the note immediately preceding the trill.

**Track 80, Example 5**

## Tremolo

The tremolo is similar to a trill, except it doesn't need to involve adjacent notes, and it may involve chords. The notation for tremolo includes the notes to be played and a bar in between that means "play these notes back and forth as fast as you can." Tremolos can be played by one hand, two hands, or alternating hands; they are found in music from Beethoven to the blues.

## Turns

Turns are graceful little figures that can occur either on the beat, or between two notes. In Baroque and early Classical music, they usually start on the upper auxiliary; in Romantic music and beyond, the starting note depends on the context.

The following example uses Ignaz Paderewski's famous "Minuet in G." The second line shows two different ways of realizing the ornaments Paderewski himself used in the first variation, as demonstrated in recordings made by the composer himself. Paderewski's version is realized on the recorded example.

**Track 81, Example 6**

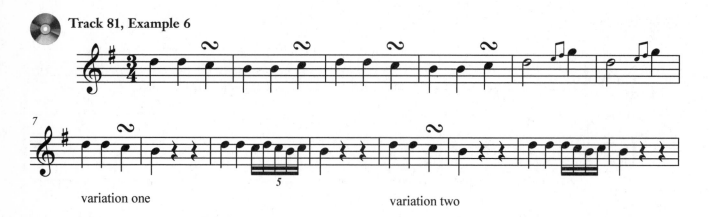

variation one                                    variation two

## Mordents

Mordents are simple three-note trills: a quick up and down, or a quick down and up, depending on how the symbol is written. Mordents are not played as triplets, but the specific duration and articulation is at the performer's discretion, according to the character of the piece. Note that the first turn starts on the principal note, whereas on the second line, the principal note is first played and briefly held before the turn starts on the upper auxiliary.

**Track 82, Example 7**

## Rolled Chords

Rolled chords are simply chords that are played one note at a time (like an arpeggio), but very quickly. As with grace notes, they all seem to be played squashed into one beat. Rolled chords allow the pianist to reach a chord that is far beyond his hand span. To roll a large chord successfully, pivot the wrist when you play the middle notes. This will extend your reach so you can get to the highest notes. When rolled chords are played with both hands, they may be played one hand at a time, or with both hands simultaneously, depending on the notation.

The lines below show three different chord scales. When playing the first line, play the chords simultaneously with both hands. For the second line, play the middle of the staff means that you play the chords at the same time. When the "roll this chord" notation is continuous, it means the hands take turns: start with the left hand and only start the right hand once the left hand has reached its top note.

## The Glissando

Finally, there is the glissando, that smashing slide that ends a passage such as a virtuosic blues improvisation.

Glissandi can be overused to the point of absurdity. Blues players seem especially susceptible to overusing this technique, but improvisers of all stripes are not immune. Remember, with ornaments, less is often more.

**FLYING FINGERS**

Here's a technique tip for the glissando: always play it as lightly as possible. Beginners tend to press down too hard on the keys, causing them to get stuck. Start by practicing on a digital keyboard (which has lighter action), then move up to an acoustic upright, and finally move up to a grand piano (which has a heavier action).

The basic technique of the glissando is to use the backs of your fingernails. To play outward (right hand ascending, left hand descending) from the center of the keyboard, you have a choice: you can play with the fingernails of the third and forth fingers, or you can turn your hand inward and use the thumbnail. To play going inward (right hand descending, left hand ascending), play with the back of the thumbnail.

 **Track 83, Example 8**

Half of the effect of a glissando is ending it with a bang—on the right note. This takes practice. You can either slide gracefully into the note (being careful not to overshoot), or you can bring your hand up just before the last note, and then hit it with some force, which works well at the end of a piece. Either strategy requires you to know which note you're going to be ending on before you get there.

 **Track 84, Example 9**

A warning about ornaments: 200 years ago, Mozart criticized his contemporaries for over-ornamenting— and 200 years later, many of us are still making the same mistake. Whether it's a cocktail pianist who overdoes the rolled chords or a bluesman who rocks out with the tremolos and the glissandi, too much of a good thing is a bad thing. Ornaments are just that—exciting little extras to spice up what you're playing. But underlying it all, there has to be musicality, expression, technique, phrasing, balance, and a sense of groove.

## The Least You Need to Know

- Ornaments are quick turns of phrase that decorate the main part of the melody.
- Ornaments contain the principal note, and may contain an upper auxiliary and the note just above the principal note and a lower auxiliary.
- If either of the auxiliary notes are to be sharp or flat, a tiny sharp or flat will be in place either above or below the ornament.
- Ornaments usually don't have their own rhythm; they are squeezed into the principal note's rhythmic value, at the taste and discretion of the performer.

# CD Table of Contents

The CD contains recordings of some of the musical examples in this book. The following list tells you which examples were recorded in which chapters. (To find the sheet music in the text, go to the pertinent chapter and look for the CD icon and track number.) In some cases, there are two or more examples on a track. In those cases, the tracks are numbered Example 1a, 1b, 1c, etc. The timing numbers—for example, Track 1b (0:13)—tells you that Track 1b starts at the 13-second mark on Track 1.

## Chapter 3

Track 1
a) Example 1: Right-hand two-finger warm-up
b) Example 2: Left-hand two-finger warm-up (0:24)

Track 2
a) Example 3: Slur exercise for fingers 1 and 2
b) Example 4: Slur exercise for fingers 2 and 3 (0:26)
c) Example 5: Slur exercise for fingers 3 and 4 (0:48)
d) Example 6: Slur exercise for fingers 4 and 5 (1:03)

Track 3
Example 7: Two-hand exercise for melody and accompaniment

## Chapter 4

Track 4
a) Example 1: Five-finger exercise for hands apart
b) Example 2: Five-finger exercise for hands together (0:38)

Track 5
a) Example 3: Chord sequence for improvisation

# Chapter 5

Track 6
a) Example 1: C Major pentascale
b) Example 2: C minor pentascale (0:08)

Track 7
Example 3: "The Erie Canal"

Track 8
Example 4: A minor pattern for transposition

Track 9
Example 5: Hands-together exercise in A minor

Track 10
Example 6: Minor key improvisation exercise

# Chapter 6

Track 11
a) Example 1: Right-hand octave jumps
b) Example 2: Left-hand octave jumps (0:27)
c) Example 3: Two-hand octave jumps in parallel motion (0:59)
d) Example 4: Two-hand octave jumps in contrary motion (1:18)

Track 12
a) Example 5: Preparatory exercise for changing positions
b) Example 6: Preparatory exercise for changing positions (0:13)
c) Example 7: Right-hand exercise for changing positions (0:27)
d) Example 8: Left-hand exercise for changing positions (0:54)
e) Example 9: Changing positions, hands together in contrary motion (1:22)
f) Example 10: Changing positions, hands together in parallel motion (1:51)

Track 13
a) Example 11: Left-hand blues bass
b) Example 12: Right-hand blues pattern (0:23)

Track 14
Example 13: Octave moves

Track 15
Example 14: Classical left-hand cadence

# Chapter 7

Track 16
Example 1: Cross-hand arpeggio in C

Track 17
Example 2: Chord inversion exercise

Track 18
Example 3: Cross-hand arpeggios in chord groups

Track 19
Example 4: Cadence in root position and voiced inversions

# Chapter 8

Track 20
Example 1: White note major scale: right hand, left hand, and together

Track 21
Example 2: Two-octave scale

Track 22
Example 3: Scales over left-hand pattern

# Chapter 9

Track 23
Example 1: C Major and A minor scales

Track 24
a) Example 2: Natural and harmonic minor scales

b) Example 3: Natural and melodic minor scales (0:09)

# Chapter 10

Track 25
Example 1: Modes in the key of C with associated chords

Track 26
Example 2: Mode cycle in C

# Chapter 11

Track 27
Example 1: Major scale and blues scale

Track 28
Example 2: Learning the blues scale

Track 29
Example 3: C, F, and G blues scales and progression

Track 30
Example 4: Alternating hands, blues shuffle

# Chapter 12

Track 31
Example 1: Chromatic scales with chord exercise

Track 32
a) Example 2: Contrary motion
b) Example 3: Parallel motion (0:09)

Track 33
a) Example 4: Whole-tone chords with sample improvisation
b) Example 5: Whole-tone chords with sample improvisation (0:26)

Track 34
Example 6: Major pentatonic scales over I–IV–V chords

# Chapter 13

Track 35
Example 1: How to play with a metronome

Track 36
Example 2: Alternating triplet and duplets

Track 37
a) Example 3: Straight eighth blues with metronome
b) Example 4: Swing blues with metronome (0:48)

Track 38
Example 5: Scale in standard, then dotted rhythms

Track 39
a) Example 6: Clementi passage
b) Example 7: Learning the passage using dotted rhythms (0:15)

Track 40
Example 8: Using rhythm to learn chord jumps

# Chapter 14

Track 41
Example 1: Dynamics exercise

Track 42
Example 2: Arpeggio dynamics

Track 43
Example 3: Chromatic scale dynamics

Track 44
Example 4: Accent on different notes of the scale

Track 45
Example 5: Legato exercise

Track 46
a) Example 6: Legato chords
b) Example 7: Legato chords (0:43)

Track 47
a) Example 8: Articulation
b) Example 9: Staccato exercise in sixths (0:16)

Track 48
Example 10: Chord articulation exercise

Track 49
Example 11: Slurs

Track 50
a) Example 12: Incorrect pedaling example
b) Example 13: Correct pedaling example (0:11)

# Chapter 15

Track 51
a) Example 1: Dynamics and hand independence, right hand louder than left hand
b) Example 2: Dynamics and hand independence, right hand with accompaniment (0:11)
c) Example 3: Dynamics and hand independence, left hand louder than right hand (0:24)
d) Example 4: Dynamics and hand independence, left-hand melody with right-hand chords (0:37)
e) Example 5: Articulation and hand independence, staccato versus legato (0:51)

Track 52
Example 6: Dynamics with call and response

Track 53
Example 7: Switching melody between hands

Track 54
Example 8: "Frere Jacques"

# Chapter 16

Track 55
a) Example 1: Finger-over-finger technique
b) Example 2: Finger-over-finger technique for chords (0:20)

Track 56
Example 3: Hand-on-hand playing

# Chapter 17

Track 57
Example 1: Basic Hanon exercise

Track 58
Example 2: Hanon with articulation

Track 59
Example 3: Hanon with different rhythms and accents

# Chapter 18

Track 60
Example 1: Chord recognition exercise

Track 61
Example 2: Waltz pattern with left-hand leaps in three different keys

Track 62
Example 3: Octaves in contrary motion

Track 63
Example 4: Cross-hand playing

# Chapter 19

Track 64
a) Example 1: Incorrectly played arpeggios
b) Example 2: Correctly played arpeggios (0:10)

Track 65
a) Example 3: Right-hand arpeggio practice
b) Example 4: Left-hand arpeggio practice (0:26)

# Chapter 20

Track 66
Example 1: Scale in thirds and sixths

Track 67
a) Example 2: Scale in broken octaves
b) Example 3: Chromatic scale in broken octaves (0:09)

Track 68
a) Example 4: Octave exercises with repeated notes
b) Example 5: Octave exercises, scale fragments (0:11)
c) Example 6: Octave exercises, scales (0:29)

# Chapter 21

Track 69
Example 1: Improvisation in 5/4 time

Track 70
a) Example 2: Two kinds of 9/8 time
b) Example 3: 9/8 time with uneven meter (0:20)

Track 71
Example 4: Uneven meter, "Pictures at an Exhibition"

Track 72
Example 5: Exercise in uneven meter

Track 73
a) Example 6: Three-against-two polyrhythm
b) Example 7: How to count three against two (0:11)

Track 74
Example 8: Exercise in 5/4 time

Track 75
a) Example 9: Three-against-four time demonstration from "Fantasie Impromptu," first slow then fast
b) Example 10: Three-against-four time demonstration (0:17)

Track 76
Example 11: Syncopation

# Chapter 22

Track 77
a) Example 1: Grace notes
b) Example 2: Grace notes with left-hand accompaniment (0:16)

Track 78
Example 3: Blues grace notes

Track 79
Example 4: Drone grace note

Track 80
Example 5: Trills

Track 81
Example 6: Turns; example from Paderewski's "Minuet in G"

Track 82
Example 7: Turns and mordents

Track 83
Example 8: Glissando

Track 84
Example 9: Blues ending with glissando and tremolo

**accent**   A sharp, flat, or natural that is added to a note.

**accidental**   A note that is not in the diatonic scale, or the sign (sharp, flat, or natural) used to signify it.

**accompaniment**   The chords and rhythmic patterns that support the melody.

**Alberti bass**   A left-hand accompaniment pattern that usually consists of a chord broken up and is played from bottom note to top note to middle note to top note.

**arpeggio**   A chord that is played one note at a time up and down the keyboard. Notes can be skipped.

**articulation**   The way in which notes are played and connected (for example, smooth and singing, or short and abrupt).

**augmented chord**   A chord that includes the first and third note of the major scale, along with the raised (sharp) fifth note.

**broken chord**   A chord that is played one note at a time, in any order.

**cadence**   A series of chords, often including the primary chords of a key.

**changes**   What jazz players call the chords in a song.

**chord**   More than two notes played together.

**chromatic notes**   Notes taken from outside the diatonic scale.

**chromatic scale**   A scale made up of all the notes on the piano, one after the other, in a series of half steps.

**comping**   Playing chords in rhythm in a jazz arrangement.

**contrary motion**   Two hands play mirror images of each other: when the left hand descends, the right hand ascends, and vice versa.

**counterpoint**   Two hands play independent voices at the same time.

**cross-hand arpeggios**   Arpeggios that are played with one hand and then the other, with the hands crossing over each other as they travel up and down the keyboard.

**diatonic**   The notes used in any major (or related minor) scale, and the chords based on those notes.

**diminished**   Lowering a note in a chord by a half step.

**diminished chord**   A minor chord with a flatted third, a diminished fifth (a half step lower than the perfect fifth), and a diminished seventh (one and a half steps below the name of the chord).

**dominant**   The fifth note in a scale.

**double octaves**   Each hand plays a series of octaves at the same time.

**dynamics**   Changes in volume.

**finger substitution**   Changing fingers on a note without playing it a second time to reach another note that would not have been possible with the first finger in its original position.

**flat**   Lowering a note by a half step.

**flatted seventh**   The seventh that is one full step below the name of the chord.

**glissando**   A technique that requires using the fingernails to sweep across the keys, from one part of the keyboard to another.

**grace notes**   Short, quick notes with no rhythmic value that are added to notes or chords for ornamentation.

**half step**   The distance from one note to the very next note on the keyboard.

**harmonic minor scale**   The minor scale with a raised seventh.

**harmony**   The chords or accompaniment.

**interval**   The distance between notes.

**inversion**   An arrangement of notes in a chord in which the root is either the middle or top note of the chord.

**inverted mordent key**   A quick trill in which the player starts on the principal note, then goes quickly down and back up again.

**key**   The tonal center of a piece of music.

**key signature**   The number of flats or sharps in a key.

**legato**   Playing notes one after the other with a smooth, connected sound; the first finger does not leave its key until the second note has sounded.

**major chord**   The chord built using the first, third, and fifth notes of the major scale.

**major seventh**   The seventh that is a half step below the name of the chord.

**major third**   A distance of two whole steps between notes.

**measure**   Notes grouped in a repeating number of beats according to the time signature.

**melodic minor scale**   A minor scale with the sixth and seventh notes raised a half step when the scale is played ascending. When the scale is played descending, the natural minor scale is played.

**melody**   The tune of a song.

**metronome**   A device that ticks to help the musician keep strict time.

**minor chord**   The chord built on the first, third, and fifth notes of the minor scale.

**minor third**   A distance of one and a half steps between notes.

**mode**   A scale that is played starting on a note other than the normal root note of the scale.

**mordent**   A quick trill between the principal note and the note immediately above it.

**natural minor scale**    The minor scale with no alterations or accidentals.

**natural sign**    An accidental indicating that a note that would normally be played sharp or flat is to be played without the sharp or the flat.

**octave**    A note that is eight notes above a note and has the same name.

**pentascale**    A five-finger pattern consisting of the first five notes of any given major or minor scale.

**pentatonic scale**    A five-note scale consisting of the first, second, third, fifth, and sixth notes of the major scale (major pentatonic), or the first, third, fourth, fifth, and seventh notes of the natural minor scale (minor pentatonic).

**polyrhythms**    A rhythmic pattern that requires one hand to divide a beat into a certain number of subdivisions, while the other hand plays a different and indivisible number of subdivisions.

**primary chords**    The most common chords, usually built on the first, fourth, and fifth degrees, in a scale.

**principal note**    The main note immediately under an ornament. The ornament is constructed in reference to this note.

**progression**    A series of chords.

**rolled chords**    A chord that is played very quickly all on one beat, the fingers playing one note at a time, in order from bottom to top.

**root position**    An arrangement of notes in a chord in which the root of the chord is the bottom note.

**scale**    A group of notes that supply most of the melodic and harmonic material in a song.

**sevenths**    The seventh note of a scale, which is added to make a chord more complex and interesting.

**sharp**    Raising a note by a half step.

**sixth**    The sixth note of a scale, which can be added to a triad.

**slur**    A marking that connects two or more notes. The notes are played legato, until the last note, after which there may be a breath or a staccato.

**sostenuto pedal**    The middle pedal that holds down only the notes that are played when it is pressed.

**staccato**    An articulation indicating that the note is to be played short, as if touching a hot stove.

**step**    Two half steps; a distance between two notes. Also called a whole step.

**sustain pedal**    The pedal on the far right, which lifts all the dampers so that the strings are free to ring.

**swing**    A style of playing in which notes may be written as eighth notes, but are played as triplets, with the first eighth note in any pair getting a longer count than the second eighth note.

**syncopation**    A rhythmic style in which the accented notes fall in between the strong beats to give the music a sense of urgency and drive.

**tempo**    The speed in which a piece is played.

**tie**    A line joining two of the same notes, indicating that the second note of the pair is to be held rather than played again.

**time signature**    The fraction or sign at the beginning of the piece that indicates how many beats are in a measure.

**tonic**    The first note in a scale.

**transpose**    To move a song from one key to another.

**tremolo**    An indication that two notes are to be played very fast. Tremolos can be applied to single notes played with one or two hands, and to chords played with one or two hands.

**triad**    A three-note chord.

**triplets**    Notes that are played in groups of three.

**turn**    An ornament that requires the pianist to play a quick series consisting of the principal note and the notes above and below the principal note.

**turnaround**    One or two measures at the end of the song that lead back to the beginning for another chorus.

**twelve-bar blues**    A traditional blues form with 12 measures following a standard chord pattern, or a variation on the standard pattern.

**una corda**    The pedal on the right, also known as the "quiet" pedal.

**voicing**    The choice a performer makes regarding how the notes in a chord are arranged.

**walking bass line**    A stepping bass pattern that often leads from one chord to another.

**whole-tone scale**    A six-note scale consisting of notes that are a whole step away from the previous notes.

Scores of composers and pedagogues have written books on various aspects of playing the piano. The list that follows is in no way complete, but it includes some of the classics that form the core of an advancing pianist's technical practice routine, along with a few particularly unusual or artistic selections. I've also included some books about piano technique.

In some cases, many editions of the exercises exist; in others, the books are out of print and hard to find. Check with online retailers for used copies.

**C. P. E. Bach.** *Essay on the True Art of Playing Keyboard Instruments.* **W.W. Norton, 1948.**
Piano technique has changed, just as pianos have changed, since Johann Sebastian Bach's mercurial son wrote this book more than 200 years ago. He gives insight into the classical style, along with information about ornamentation.

**Oscar Beringer.** *Daily Technical Studies for the Pianoforte.* **Kalmus Edition, 1999.**
Oscar Beringer's text covers finger independence, chord and scale passages, hand crossings, extensions, and wrist and finger action, with exercises designed to be played in all keys. This is not a book for beginners.

**Seymour Bernstein.** *20 Lessons in Keyboard Choreography.* **Seymour Bernstein Music, 1991.**
Seymour Bernstein emphasizes connecting musical feeling with physical action, and attention to finger, hand, wrist, and arm movements.

**Olga and Leon Conus.** *Fundamentals of Piano Technique.* **Alfred Publishing, 1994.**
This edition is a republication of Olga and Leon Conus's 1954 two-volume set of exercises. The original cover boasted the endorsing signatures of Horowitz, Arrau, and Casadesus. These exercises emphasize isolating individual technical elements to enable the player to play without tension.

**J. B. Cramer.** *50 Selected Piano Studies.* **Schirmer, 1967.**
These highly musical etudes are appropriate for advanced students.

**Carl Czerny.** *School of Velocity, Op. 299: (Complete) Piano Technique.* **Snowball Publishing, 2010.**
Carl Czerny, a student of Beethoven's, devoted his composing life to writing piano exercises. This is his most famous.

**Seymour Fink.** *Mastering Piano Technique: A Guide for Students, Teachers and Performers.* **Amadeus Press, 2003.**
Seymour Fink provides a holistic guide to the keyboard, emphasizing technique as a means for musical expression and interpretation.

**Heinrich Gebhard.** *The Art of Pedaling: A Manual for the Use of the Piano Pedals.* **F. Colombo, 1963.**
This 450-page guide covers an oft-neglected area of technique: the pedals.

**Walter Gieseking and Karl Leimer.** *Piano Technique.* **Dover Publications, 1972.**
This volume combines two books by one of the mid-twentieth century's towering pianists and his renowned teacher: *The Shortest Way to Pianistic Perfection* and *Rhythmics, Dynamics, Pedal and Other Problems of Piano Playing.*

**Charles Louis Hanon.** *Virtuoso Pianist in Sixty Exercises for the Piano.* **G. Schirmer, 1986.**
The classic exercises.

**Stephen Heller.** *Selected Piano Studies, Opus 45 and 46.* **G. Schirmer, 2005.**
A contemporary and friend of Schumann, Liszt, and Chopin, Stephen Heller composed etudes that were both musical and technical. Opus 45 and 46 are his most famous.

**Maurice Hinson.** *Technique for the Advancing Pianist.* **Alfred Publishing, 2004.**
This text covers scales, chords, and arpeggios, along with exercises for developing precision, speed, agility, and tone.

**Gerald Klickstein.** *The Musician's Way: A Guide to Practice, Performance, and Wellness.* **Oxford University Press, 2009.**
There isn't a note of music in this volume, but there is a world of information about how to effectively practice to develop technique.

**Josef Pischna.** *Technical Studies—Sixty Progressive Exercises for the Piano.* **G. Schirmer, 1986.**
Josef Pischna provides a multi-key approach to technique with exercises for articulation, dynamics, rhythm, and tempo written in every key.

**Aloys Schmitt.** *Op. 16: Preparatory Exercises for the Piano.* **G. Schirmer, 1986.**
Often used as an alternative to the Hanon exercises, these drills work on finger independence.

**Robert Schultz and Tina Faigen.** *Accelerando Series (Piano Technique Series).* **FJH Music Company, 2006.**
This seven-volume series covers technique from elementary through late-intermediate playing.

# Index

# F

## T

## U-V

## W-X-Y-Z